HAND-STITCHED
QUILTS

Dedication

For all the unnamed stitchers who came before us,
leaving us their hand-stitched quilts to inspire
and admire.

First published in 2023
Search Press Limited
Wellwood, North Farm Road,
Tunbridge Wells, Kent TN2 3DR

Reprinted 2023

Text and templates copyright © Carolyn Forster 2023

PHOTOGRAPHY
Pages 22 (T), 106 (R), 108, 109, 110, 118, 126, 128 by Paul Bricknell
All remaining photographs by Mark Davison
Styling by Marrianne Miall
Illustrations on pages 36–88 and 97–101 by Bess Harding
Photographs, illustrations and design copyright
© Search Press Ltd. 2023

ISBN: 978-1-78221-671-1
ebook ISBN: 978-1-78126-586-4

The Publishers and author can accept no responsibility for any
consequences arising from the information, advice or instructions
given in this publication.

SUPPLIERS

For details of suppliers, please visit the Search Press website:
www.searchpress.com

BOOKMARKED

Extra copies of the templates are also available to download free
from the Bookmarked Hub: www.bookmarkedhub.com

Search for this book by title or by ISBN number; the files can be
found under 'Book Extras'. Membership of the Bookmarked online
community is free.

MEASUREMENTS & CONVERSIONS

The projects in this book have been made using imperial
measurements, and the metric equivalents provided have been
calculated following standard conversion practices. The metric
measurements are often rounded to the nearest 0.25cm for ease
of use except in rare circumstances; however, if you need more
exact measurements, there are a number of excellent online
converters that you can use. Always use either metric or imperial
measurements, not a combination of both.

ABOUT THE AUTHOR

For more information about Carolyn Forster and her work, visit:

▶ her website – www.carolynforster.co.uk

▶ her Instagram page – @quiltingonthego

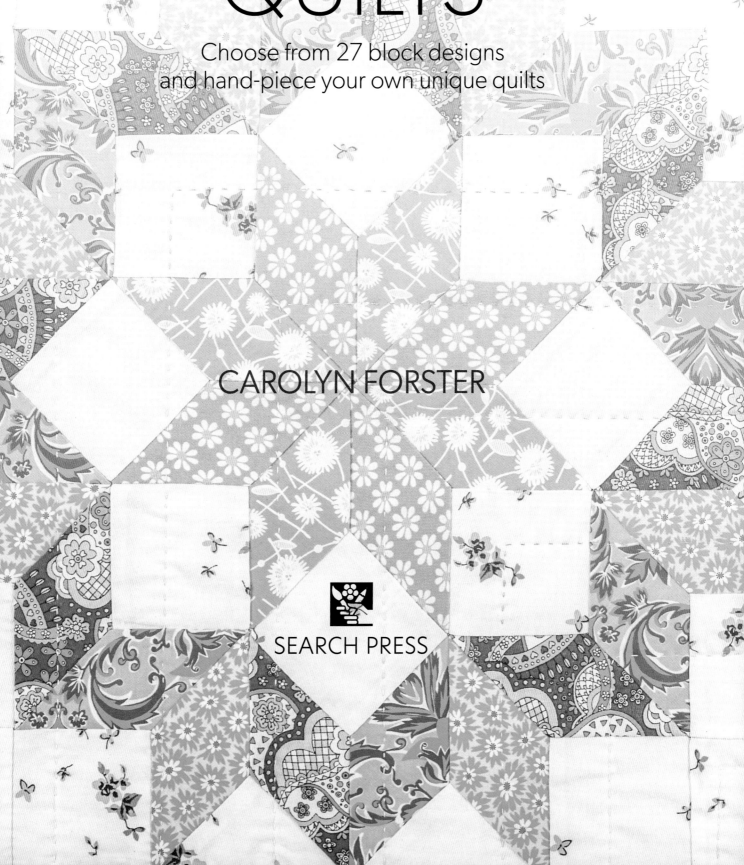

HAND-STITCHED
QUILTS

Choose from 27 block designs
and hand-piece your own unique quilts

CAROLYN FORSTER

SEARCH PRESS

CONTENTS

THE **BLOCKS**

INTRODUCTION

'Start where you are, use what you have and do what you can.'

Arthur Ashe, based on a quote by Theodore Roosevelt

When I meet students who want to start to stitch a quilt, they often talk about the things that they feel are stopping them: does it matter if they don't have a sewing machine, will sewing by hand be durable enough and how long will it take to make a quilt by hand?

Let's think about the antique and vintage quilts that might have inspired us to want to start stitching our own, then pause to think about the lives of the (mostly) women who made them. Often a household would have had needle and thread at the least for repairs, and fabric scraps from old clothes or dressmaking. This is all you need to start making a patchwork quilt by hand. Don't let the tech get in the way of starting out on a sewing adventure.

Is it OK to sew by hand?

I have always hand stitched patchwork pieces, as that was how I learnt. The process was a contrast to the work in garment making that I was doing on the machine, so I enjoyed the change of pace. The fact that I could stitch in peace and quiet, or choose to watch the TV and stitch, appealed to me too. When I did start sewing quilts on the sewing machine, I enjoyed the speed with which things came together, and the different methods and approaches that the machine offered. I soon realized, though, that while some patchwork blocks do just go together better on the machine, others are actually easier by hand. I realized also that because I had two sets of skills – one for hand piecing and one for machine piecing – it was easy to work out which blocks to make depending on time and whether I had access to the sewing machine.

Do I need a machine to sew a quilt?

Having a sewing machine is not a prerequisite to making patchwork. You might eventually have to buy or have access to a machine, but you don't need one to start sewing patchwork. Hand stitching started before people stitched quilts, and quilts were stitched before people had access to sewing machines.

Many of the blocks in this book can be made by machine. It is easy to combine the two methods – hand sewing blocks and then adding sashing by machine, for example. But there is no reason why sashing can't be added by hand also.

There are lots of things to enjoy about hand sewing your quilt in its entirety. For starters, if you don't own a machine then learning to sew the patchwork and then quilting it by hand, and even finishing it by hand, allows you to join in with the creativity of thousands of other people today and connect you with the social and historical side of an embedded cultural experience. You just need a needle, thread and scissors.

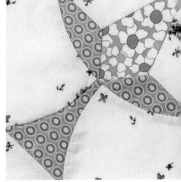

If you do own a sewing machine, then sometimes taking a step away from that for some of your projects will open you up to a new way of viewing your quilt making. Quilt making by hand requires a different approach and a different set of guidelines. It can often make the sewing process easier and more straightforward, and it will show you a different set of problem-solving skills that may help you approach your machine sewing in a different way.

Is it slower to stitch a quilt by hand?

Let me get this out of the way early on. Sewing by hand is not slower than sewing on a machine. If you have access to your machine and can sit and sew at it then you will be faster than a hand-piecer sitting next to you. But you can only sew on it when you sit at it. A hand-piecer can stitch anywhere anytime. Hand stitching is portable and social.

You can stitch with family and friends while watching TV; or at the sports ground, waiting for practice sessions to end. You can stitch in waiting rooms, while travelling, and while having coffee with non-stitching friends. You can stitch quietly on your own, at your own pace and enjoying your own peace; or you can join a group of stitching friends to sew and chat and enjoy each other's company.

Learning to hand piece your patchwork can open up a personal time and space that is often needed with today's frenetic lifestyles. Being able to just sit and stitch, and concentrate on that, allows us to immerse ourselves in the process and often lose ourselves in that moment. As you stitch over time, you build up a rhythm of working, and with that it is easy to let thoughts wander and distil. It gives you a chance to get lost in your thoughts, and this can be viewed as a therapeutic benefit of hand stitching. You can allow stresses to be let go as your mind focuses on the task in hand, and often a new creativity is born from this.

In a way, piecing and quilting by hand gives us guilt-free time with our own mind. After all, you are making/doing something at the same time. By taking the time to sew by hand, you are renewing your patience and showing yourself that actually, this isn't taking as long as you thought it would. That in itself is a refreshing thought. The process turns out to be as rewarding as the end product.

I teach both machine and hand pieced patchwork, and one of the biggest contrasts in these classes is the pace and atmosphere – or 'vibe', if you like. The conversations that are started, the world being put to right, or confidences shared; generally, we come out of these classes feeling refreshed and ready for the rest of the day, something that benefits everyone.

How to read this book

When you begin hand piecing, you can work through the blocks in the book. Start with the simpler ones and then move onto those that require more skill. As your skills progress, you will see that some blocks could be easier to make on the sewing machine, but some offer new challenges and are, in fact, better worked by hand – for example, the set-in seams of Drusilla's Delight (see page 68). If you choose to buy a sewing machine at some point and learn the techniques for machine piecing and quilting, that is great! Like many quilters before you, they started by hand, liked what they saw and invested in a machine to add new skills and techniques to their skill base.

But you will always have a choice: by having the skill base of hand work, you have given yourself the choice to work in whichever way is most comfortable to you wherever you are and however you feel.

QUILT MATERIALS

All the blocks in this book are designed to be pieced together to make a sampler quilt. The finished quilt size is 72½in (184.25cm) square. To make the quilt, you will need the following items.

Patchwork blocks

For the two different sampler quilts I stitched in this book (see pages 94 and 95), I used a scrappy combination of fabrics. You may wish to start with a themed group of fabrics to give you your direction and help make the choices easier along the way. I suggest you start off with four or five Fat Quarters (or quarter metres) of fabrics that you like together and then, as you make your way through the blocks, introduce more fabrics. One way to ease yourself into a scrap quilt is to decide on 16 fabrics (as there are 16 units in the quilt) and take it from there. Again, add new fabrics as needed, but starting with a small selection will help you control the colourway.

Background fabric

You will need 144in (3.75m) x WOF (width of fabic – this is a standard 40in (101.5cm) wide bolt). Note that this amount is generous.

This fabric is the off-white fabric seen in nearly all of the patchwork blocks. It gives the quilt continuity and helps show off the print fabrics and block designs. I have used one fabric, but there is nothing to stop you using different fabrics throughout the quilt.

You could take a scrappy approach with your background fabric, and use a different one for the back of each block. I would allow one Fat Quarter (22 x 18in or 55 x 45.75cm) of fabric for each block. Some blocks will use less, and some will use all of it. As you work your way through the blocks, you can introduce more fabrics or use up what you have remaining.

Backing

For our quilt, you will need 164in (4.25m) x WOF (40in or 101.5cm). Then cut this into two equal lengths. Remove the selvedge/selvage (see page 18) and stitch together along the length with a ⅜in (1cm) seam allowance. Press the seam allowance open.

Wadding/batting

You will need an 82in (208cm) square.

Binding

You will need 36in (91.5cm) x WOF (40in or 101.5cm). Cut eight strips measuring 4½in (11.5cm) wide x WOF. Join the strips with a bias join (see page 123) to create a continuous length. Trim the seam allowance to ¼in (5mm) and press open. Press along the entire length, with the wrong sides together.

PIECING MATERIALS

FABRIC

I find it easier to stitch with 100 per cent cotton fabrics that are dress/craft weight. But if you are just starting out or keen to recycle worn clothing, then you could use some old clothes in your patchwork. This adds a nice touch, personalizing the process and the end result. If you prefer to work with fabric with a little more body, then I would recommend using a spray starch product. This spritz will add body, but still be easy to stitch, and will stabilize the fabric when you are drawing on it.

If you are using newly bought fabrics, pre-wash them to minimize colour bleed or transfer and shrinkage. Press flat before cutting the fabric.

THREAD

The colours that most patchwork can be stitched with will be an uninspiring set of basic 'shadow' like colours. The reason for this is you need them to merge with the fabric. Colours that will be useful are:

- cream
- dark cream
- light grey
- dark grey
- navy
- black
- tan
- sludgy grey/green.

I tend to use 100 per cent cotton thread, as the fabrics I use are usually made of cotton. I buy thread in the most economical way I can, which is to buy it on large spools. As I only use a limited number of colours for piecing patchwork, this makes sense. If I need the work to be portable, then I buy the small spools for ease of carrying. I only use these when I stitch outside of the house. If you have a sewing machine you can always wind a bobbin of thread and then use that to travel with.

The weight of thread that I like to hand piece with is Aurifil 28wt. I like the feel of it when I sew and the handle of it in the needle. You may prefer something closer to a machine piecing-weight cotton like the Aurifil 40wt or Aurifil 50wt. It's always worth trying different thread weights to see which one you prefer. Note that different brands will handle differently too.

CUTTING & SEWING
FABRIC

All the shapes in this book are cut using templates, although several could be achieved with rotary cutting. Each method will have its own advantages, and it's worth considering both to see what works best for you in your situation.

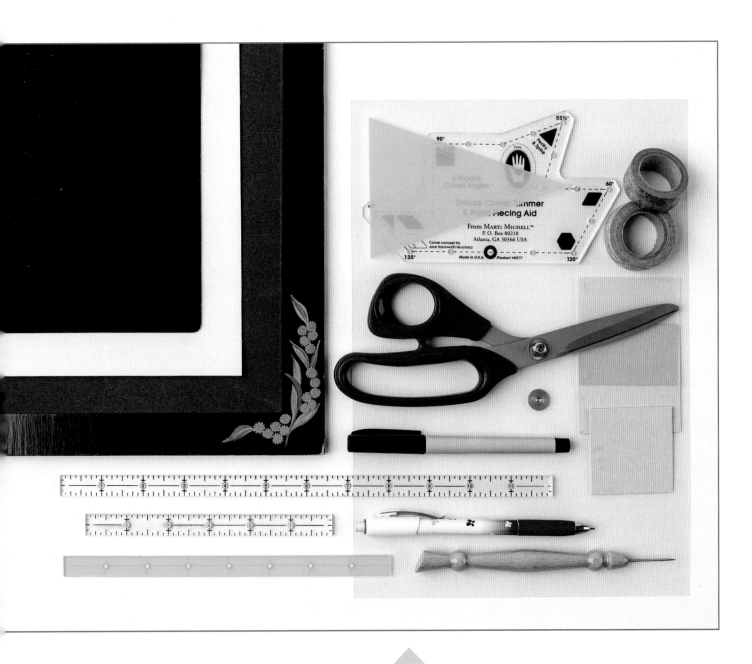

EQUIPMENT

Paper-cutting scissors

For cutting templates, card and plastic. These should be comfortable to handle with a sharp blade. In some cases, these may be scissors that were once fabric-only scissors, but they became dull or developed a nick, so aren't great on fabric anymore. Most sewists will have separate scissors for fabric, and then a pair for everything else, to keep their fabric scissors in top condition.

Fabric cutting scissors

If you are using templates then you need good scissors. Use a pair that are not too big for your hand and that you feel in control of. My favourite scissors for cutting the patches are ones with a slightly serrated edge. These seem to grip the fabric as you cut and allow for nice precise work.

Rulers & tools

Your basic rotary cutter rulers are all useful for marking a ¼in (5mm) seam allowance (SA) when needed, especially the smaller sizes as they are easier to handle. I use the following rotary-cutting ruler sizes: ½ x 6in (1.25 x 15.25cm), 1 x 6in (2.5 x 15.25cm) and 1 x 12in (2.5 x 30.5cm). There are also specific tools whose sole purpose is to draw a sewing line on fabric shapes that include the SA. If you have cut squares, triangles and rectangles that include the SA using the rotary cutter or a die-cutting machine, then these tools help you mark in your sewing line accurately. Products include:

▸ Quick Quarter
▸ Quilters Quarter Bar
▸ Fons & Porter Quarter Inch Seam Markers
▸ Perfect Piecer by Jinny Beyer
▸ Deluxe Corner Trimmer and Hand Piecing Aid
  by Marti Michell.

Pens and pencils

A propelling pencil designed for fabric is a good choice as it will always be sharp.

Templates

See pages 130–144 for the full-size templates, and pages 12–17 for details on making and using templates.

Magic Seam Marker by Sew Easy®

See page 16.

Rotary cutter

Like a pizza wheel, a rotary cutter cuts through up to about eight layers of fabric at a time. Keep the blade sharp and free of nicks, and cut through as many or as few layers as you are comfortable with.

Self-healing cutting mat

This purpose-made mat is available from craft and patchwork stores and is used in conjunction with a rotary cutter and rotary-cutting rulers or templates for cutting fabric. It is marked into a grid that you can use to help you measure and cut the fabric in straight lines. Buy the largest size you can afford so you will not have to fold your fabric so much.

Non-slip surfaces

▸ If you want to have templates that do not slip then it is possible to add some sandpaper dots to the back of them, which will grip the fabric.

▸ You can also use repositionable spray glue like 404 which will make the back of the shape tacky.

▸ To ensure you draw round the templates on the wrong side of the fabric as accurately as possible, you can put the fabric onto a sheet of sandpaper. When you draw on it, the pencil will not drag on the fabric.

▸ Some people find that using spray starch on the fabric gives it more stability, and lessens any drag.

▸ For others, just having the fabric on a cutting mat is enough to stop the fabric dragging.

▸ Other options to consider are the reversible Design Mats. These soft mats grip the table and the fabric, so that neither slip. The fabric should not drag when you draw on them.

▸ I have also used a square of Roc-lon Multi-Purpose cloth. This can be brought from craft and sewing shops and cut to size. The gritty fabric will grip the fabric as you draw.

TEMPLATE MATERIALS

Card

The quickest and easiest way for many of us to use the templates in this book is to photocopy the shapes and glue them to firm card. These can then be cut out, ready to use.

This is fine if you do not want to use the template for more than a few blocks. Each time you draw round it the edges will soften, and the shape will change a little over a period of use. You can draw around them with pencil, and sometimes with continued usage this will stain the card, which in turn may transfer to fabric when you don't want it to.

I use card for single-use templates when I quickly want to get an idea of how the block will turn out.

Perspex/acrylic

Some shapes in the template section may be available as ready-made acrylic templates. Most commonly these will be squares, rectangles and triangles. Some more unusual shapes can be found too, as seen below (Turkey Tracks template set). Bear in mind that these templates will include the seam allowance (SA), and you will need to draw in a sewing line. These acrylic templates are useful if you'll be using them a lot. The advantage of these shapes is that you will be able to cut round them with a rotary cutter, making the cutting process quicker.

Plastic

This is a more durable option when making your own templates. Most patchwork and quilting shops will sell transparent plastic sheets. You can trace templates onto them with a permanent marker pen, and you can glue photocopied patterns to them too. They are easy to cut accurately with paper scissors. I use template plastic for the majority of my templates.

Some template plastic sheets have a graph printed on them. You might find these useful for certain shapes – such as squares, rectangles and triangles – as they will make it easier to trace because there are fewer lines to draw. You can measure the shapes and work out on the grid the size of the piece to cut.

If you have traced the templates and then find it hard to see the drawn line when you hold the transparent plastic up to cut (**A**), stick a piece of masking tape behind the line so that you have some contrast, and then peel it away when the shape is cut (**B**). I cut out on the fine line that I have drawn. If the line is thicker, you may want to cut out inside the line so as not to increase the size of the shape at this stage.

If you trace the templates, remember to add information to each piece (like the grain line) and any instructions on the shape you have traced (which block it belongs to, and how many to cut). You can do this directly onto the template (**C**) or, if it is easier to see, write on an adhesive label and then stick this on the template.

Tips

▸ Many pattern designers working with patchwork blocks that have unusual pattern structures produce Perspex/acrylic template sets for these shapes. They can be used with the rotary cutter and, depending on the designer, they will have the SA marked on and holes in the templates for you to mark the fabric.

▸ Templates, and even fabric, can be cut with a variety of die-cutting machines that are on the market, with cutting plates that include the SA. This method allows you to cut multiples too.

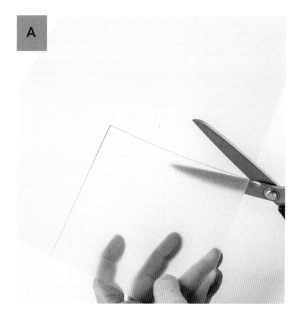

A

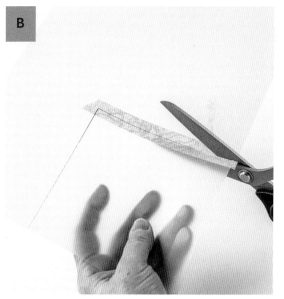

B

C

USING TEMPLATES

All of the templates at the back of this book, on pages 130–144, do not include the seam allowance (SA) and are the actual finished size of the patchwork piece (patch). When you transfer and cut out the templates from your chosen material, you can decide whether they will include the SA (this is the standard ¼in or 5mm), or whether to keep them at the finished size of the actual patch and add the SA when you cut them from the fabric.

If your template is the finished size, when you draw around it on the fabric this will be your sewing line. You will then add the SA when you cut it out, and this can be done by eye, with no added measuring. If your template includes the SA, when you cut it out you may need to add the sewing line, depending on your skill level.

If you need help deciding whether to include the SAs or not, carefully read the information on the next few pages.

How to use templates successfully

▸ Measure the template for sizing against the original after you have copied or traced it to ensure accuracy.

▸ When drawing round the template, use a fine sharp pencil. Propelling pencils work well as they are always sharp.

▸ Angle the pencil in towards the template, not away from it, so as not to make the shape larger.

▸ Cut out the fabric along the drawn line if the template includes the SA, so as not to make the shape bigger or smaller.

▸ Check the original template against the drawn-in line of your fabric shape, especially if the template does not include an SA.

Hold the pencil at an angle, towards the template, to achieve a more accurate drawn line.

Templates without the SA

These kinds of templates are the finished size of the patch you want to sew. Templates without a SA work well with curved or unusually shaped templates (such as the Thirties Tulip block on page 86).

Leave a decent-sized gap between the patches/templates to add the SA.

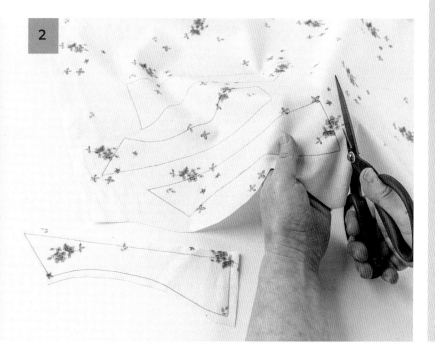

Why would I use this method?

This method means that you will always have the sewing line drawn onto the back of the fabric. This is often useful when you start hand piecing patchwork, as it means the pieces will be accurate, and most of us will start sewing this way.

METHOD

1 Draw around the shape with a sharp or propelling pencil on the back of the fabric. You should leave a good amount of space between each shape to allow you to add the SA when you cut out the shape.

2 When you cut out the shape, add the ¼in (5mm) SA. It does not need to be drawn on or measured exactly; I eyeball the cutting. If you are uncertain to start with, always cut the SA bigger. You can always trim this down as needed, but you can't add on the SA if you cut too narrowly. Because you pin along the drawn sewing line (see below), if the patches have an uneven SA it does not matter as you are not matching this up. It can be trimmed evenly later if need be.

3 To sew the patches together, begin by pinning them right sides together along the sewing lines that you drew on both patches.

4 When you stitch you will be following the drawn line, so you have a clear guide as to when to start and stop sewing.

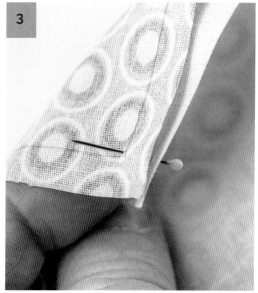

Adding a SA to your templates

This method will open up more ways to cut the fabrics, and may save more fabric too as you can place your templates closer together.

The SA can be added easily to straight-sided shapes, as you draw them onto the plastic or card using a rotary-cutting ruler. I find the ½ x 6in (1.25 x 15.25cm), 1 x 6in (2.5 x 15.25cm) and the 1 x 12in (2.5 x 30.5cm) rulers really useful for this. If you want to cut templates for unusual shapes that may include curves, then you will need to use a two-step process – see right.

1 Transfer then cut out the template from a piece of paper at the finished size. Then place it on top of the template card or plastic. You may want to secure it with some double-sided tape to stop it moving.

2 Now draw around it using a Magic Seam Marker®. This is a metal wheel that has a hole in the centre. Put the pencil in the hole and draw it round the shape. The new drawn line is ¼in (5mm) bigger than the original shape. Cut out the new shape and label accordingly.

KNOWING WHERE TO SEW THE SEAM LINE

When the shape has the SA included, there will be no line on the back of your fabric patch to follow once you have cut them out. If you are new to hand piecing, I recommend drawing in a stitch line so you have something to follow when you sew your pieces together.

There are different tools to help you with this, and all can be marked with a pencil. They are listed on page 11, under 'Rulers and tools'.

Remember also that you need only to mark the fabric patch that is facing you as you sew. You do not need to mark the other fabric patch, as you will be matching up the raw edges of the fabric to align the patches.

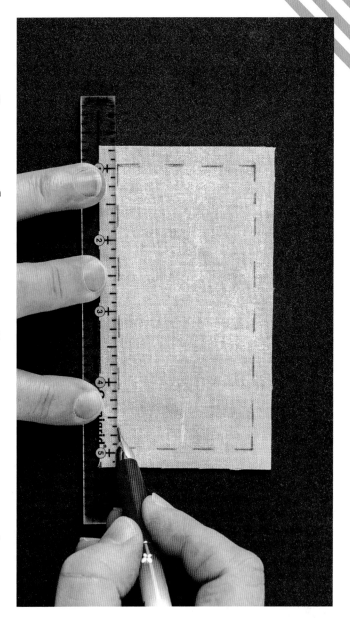

1 Simply place your chosen ruler on top of the cut fabric shape, on the wrong side (WS) of the fabric, and line it up so that you can draw a solid or dashed line that is ¼in (5mm) from the raw edge (see image right). You will need to mark all of the sides that will be sewn, including the corners, so that you know where to start and stop.

2 To sew two patches together, match up the cut edge of the two pieces, with the WS of the marked patch facing you, then pin along the sewing line. The two cut edges will line up and the sewing line will be ¼in (5mm) away from the edge.

As you become more experienced you will not need to mark a solid or dashed line – as long as the corners are marked, you can just mark dots to sew along. The tools by Jinny Beyer and Marti Michell both help with this as they have dots drilled into the rulers.

Eventually, with experience, you will be able to eyeball a seam line and no longer need to mark it in.

Why would I use this method?

This method can allow for multiple patches to be cut, and so often will quicken the process.

As you become more experienced in sewing patches, you will not actually need the sewing line to follow. Nowadays, if I have used templates that include the SA, I can stitch all of my pieces without a line to follow. This may sound alarming when you are first starting out, but with practice you will be there sooner than you think.

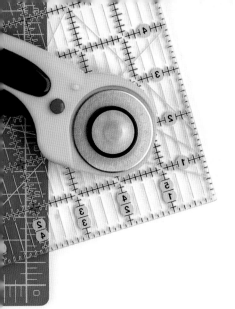

CUTTING FABRIC

If you decide to cut some of your shapes with the seam allowance (SA) included, using your rotary cutter, ruler and cutting mat, the following will make the process easier.

Note that all the steps on these pages assume you are right-handed and work from left to right; if you are left-handed, work from right to left.

Trimming the fabric for grain-line cutting

Even if you are using pre-cut fabric, such as Fat Quarters, I recommend checking and trimming your fabric as instructed below to ensure your shapes are cut flat and go together neatly.

You could use this method to prepare your fabrics for sashing strips and post squares (see page 90), and for cutting your binding strips (see page 122).

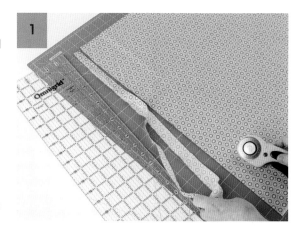

1 Hold up the fabric with the two selvedges/selvages together to see if the fabric is twisted. If it is, move the fabric in your hands to straighten it out. (When the fabric is on the grain, there should be no shifting when you pull down on it.) This will often mean that the cut edges are now not even, but these will be trimmed off soon. Fold the fabric in half lengthwise and lay it on the cutting mat, with the selvedge on a horizontal line closest to you and the fold along the top. Align the ruler with one of the vertical lines on the cutting mat and trim off the uneven fabric along the cross grain (the edge that is parallel to the cut edge of the fabric bolt), about ¾in (2cm) in from the side. Hold the ruler in place throughout the cutting process, and push the cutter away from you. Keeping the cutter pressed firmly against the ruler as you go will help create a straight, even edge.

2 If you're cutting strips for borders or binding, you could cut these out now before cutting out your template shapes, to ensure you have enough fabric to complete your quilt. Along the trimmed edge, place the ruler at your desired width – here it's 2½in (6.5cm). Cut out your strip.

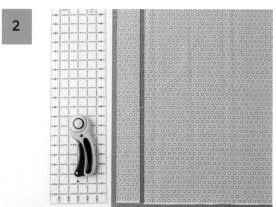

3 To fix the uneven selvedge/cross grain edge, move the fabric or strip over a horizontal line on your cutting mat until you can trim an even edge with no selvedge. Cut off the raw edge/selvedge, with the cutter moving away from you. Lift up the ruler and remove the trimmed off piece.

4 You can pile up to eight layers of fabric together if you're rotary cutting, but you will need a sharp blade and a firm hand. Work with as many or as few layers as you are comfortable with!

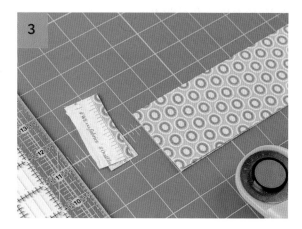

Cutting without templates

Some of the shapes in this book that could be rotary cut include squares, rectangles, strips, Half Square Triangles (HSTs) and Quarter Square Triangles (QSTs). Follow these basic guidelines for cutting fabric with the SA included, based on the templates in this book.

SQUARES

1 Measure the sides of the template – e.g. 2 x 2in (5 x 5cm).

2 Now add the ¼in (5mm) SA for each side (¼ + ¼ = ½) – e.g. 2 + ½ = 2½in (6.5cm).

3 Cut strips using this figure, then sub-cut into squares that include the SA – e.g. cut strips measuring 2½in (6.5cm) that are then sub-cut into 2½in (6.5cm) squares.

RECTANGLES

1 Measure the side of the template – e.g. 2 x 4in (5 x 10cm).

2 Now add the ¼in (5mm) SA for each side (¼ + ¼ = ½) – e.g. (2 + ½) x (4 + ½) = 2½ x 4½in (6.5 x 11.5cm).

3 Cut strips using the width figure, then sub-cut into rectangles that include the SA – e.g. cut strips measuring 2½in (6.5cm) wide then sub-cut into 2½in x 4½in (6.5 x 11.5cm) rectangles.

HALF-SQUARE TRIANGLES (HST)

1 Measure the side of the template showing the straight of grain line – e.g. 2in (5cm).

2 Now add ⅞in (2.25cm) SA – e.g. 2 + ⅞ = 2⅞in (7.25cm).

3 Cut strips using this figure, then sub-cut into squares that include the SA – e.g. cut strips 2⅞in (7.25cm) wide then sub-cut into 2⅞in (7.25cm) squares.

4 Cut each square diagonally once to make two triangles.

QUARTER-SQUARE TRIANGLES (HST)

1 Measure the side of the template showing the straight of grain – e.g. 2in (5cm).

2 Now add the 1¼in (3.25cm) SA – e.g. 2 + 1¼ = 3¼in (8.25cm).

3 Cut strips using this figure, then sub-cut into squares that include the SA – e.g. cut strips measuring 3¼in (8.25cm) wide then sub-cut 3¼in (8.25cm) squares.

4 Cut each square diagonally twice to make four triangles.

EQUIPMENT FOR HAND PIECING

Hand piecing your patchwork requires very little basic equipment. Once the patches have been cut, to sew them together you will need just needles, pins, sewing thread and possibly thimbles.

Not everyone will stitch in the same way or use the same equipment. If you are happy with the results simply using the things you have, that is great. But it is always worth trying something new or different to stitch. You never know what that new experience might offer. Remember: 'If you do what you always do, you will get what you always get.'

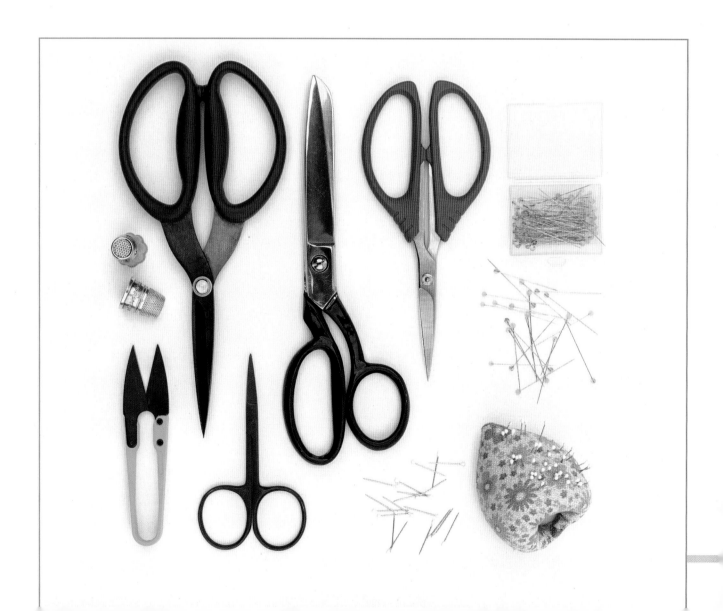

Scissors

For fabric, use a pair that you are happy to hold in your hand and that you feel you have control over. I like the scissors with a serrated edge to the blade as they do not slip, and they seem to grip the fabric as they cut.

For thread, use a small pair of scissors or thread snips for the sole purpose of cutting the sewing thread. These will stop you getting dull points in a larger pair of fabric-cutting scissors, and for most people these will be easier to handle and more portable.

Needles

Sew with a needle you are comfortable with and that will hold the thread without coming out of the eye when you stitch. The needle should pull through the fabric easily with no tugging needed. A good general needle, such as a Sharps size 10, will work well for most people.

I have also used a quilting (Betweens) needle in size 10 to piece with, as I tend to have a few of these to hand. You can buy special piecing needles for patchwork that are longer than regular needles, and these will need a different sewing action when using them due to their length.

Whatever needle you use, you should be able to thread the needle easily. Lots of brands produce needles with easy-threading or long eyes to make it easier for you.

Marking tools

I recommend using a fine propelling pencil, as this will always give you a clear fine line. Propelling pencils do not need sharpening, and often they come in a selection of colours so that one will show up on your fabric. You could use a regular pencil with a hard lead, if that's what you have.

Pins

For me there are two routes to go down on the pin front. One is long and fine, the other is short and neat. Either way, it is worth investing in a quality pin that is sharp as this will help with the accuracy of pinning the patches together.

The pins I use the most are the Clover (Short) Appliqué Pins or the Clover Patchwork Pins.

Thimbles

These are often the most controversial tools of hand sewing. I did not always use a thimble: I braved out the sore fingers and chipped nails until I had to do something. I went through all of the finger protectors on the market – the tape, the dots the finger sheaths and wraps. And they all helped. They all basically got me used to wearing something on the end of my fingers to make the sewing process easier, quicker and less painful.

Eventually, I realized that I could sew with a dimpled metal thimble on my right-hand middle finger (used to push the needle along) and a ridged flat-top thimble on my left-hand index finger (the fabric is held over the ridge of the thimble, then the needle is pushed against this to make the stitches).

So, thimbles will make things easier, but you need to get used to them if you don't already use them. You may need to travel different finger-protector routes to get there.

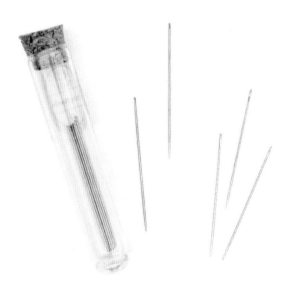

STARTING TO **STITCH**

Here are some good things to know and helpful tips to bear in mind
when you begin your hand piecing.

BEFORE YOU BEGIN

Read through all the instructions for each block before you
start. Make sure you have all the materials and equipment
you need, and that you are familiar with the techniques used.
For the designs in this book:

▸ all seam allowances (SA) are ¼in (5mm) unless otherwise
stated. But you will mainly be eyeballing this when you
cut out your fabric patches

▸ all fabric cut off the bolt is cut across the width, unless
otherwise stated

▸ all fabric quantities are based on a 40in (101.5cm)
useable width of fabric or bolt (WOF)

▸ 'WS' means the wrong side of the fabric; 'RS' means the
right side of the fabric.

Length of thread

Cut the thread to the length of your arm. Hold the end of the
thread between your thumb and index finger, and unwind
the spool with your other hand until it hits your shoulder. This
is the length to cut. This length results in fewer knots, better
tension and consistent stitches, but also encourages the most
ergonomic, rhythmic sewing action, as you pull the thread
from the pivot point of your elbow.

Starting and ending a stitch

I've found the following technique the most secure way for
starting and ending a stitch when piecing.

1 Tie a knot at one end of a length of thread as long as your arm
(see above). Thread the free end into the needle.

2 You will start to stitch with a knot and a backstitch; when you
finish stitching, end with two or three backstitches.

Threading a needle

When threading a needle, I always find it easier to
hold the thread and put the needle over it, rather
than trying to poke the thread through the needle's
eye. If you find threading the needle difficult,
invest in a needle threader, or easy-thread needles.

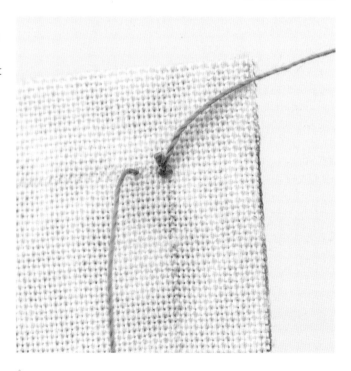

GENERAL TIPS FOR
RUNNING-STITCH SEWING

Running stitches are used for sewing all the pieces together. Although running stitch is fairly self-explanatory, there are some subtle nuances of stitching that may help make things easier, or give you a better tension to your line of stitching.

How many stitches to the inch?

This is something I have never really worried about or counted, but as I often get asked this question I did look at some of my seams and count. I stitch roughly nine stitches every 1in (2.5cm), which means five on the top and four on the back. This can vary depending on the fabric and where I am stitching, so don't take it as something to aim for!

What you are looking for, though, is not quantity but quality. The stitches need to be firm enough so that, if you pull the seam open, you shouldn't see daylight through the gaps. This will all come with practice, and having the right tension in the seam.

How to stitch

Work small running stitches, making a backstitch every 1in (2.5cm) or so to help secure your seam.

Stitching tips

▶ You do not have to pick up and pull through each stitch. You can gather up two, three or four on the needle and then pull through (**A**).

▶ Think about how you put the needle through the fabric. I find it easier to have the fabric taut over the edge of the ridged thimble on my underneath hand, and then use this finger to push the fabric onto the needle (**B**). This way, the needle is kept flat and almost stationary. The middle finger of my top hand is then basically being pushed against until I pull the needle through. It is a bit like gathering the fabric up on the needle.

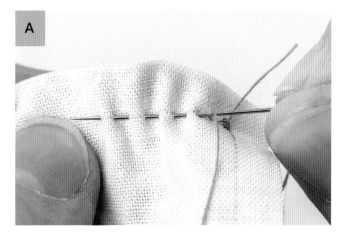

Scooping several stitches at a time before pulling through.

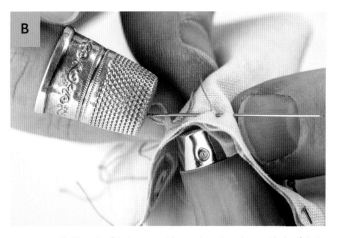

Pulling the fabric taut with one hand underneath the fabric, and pushing the fabric on top onto the needle.

▸ Something that makes long seams easier to sew is putting them under tension. You might have seen or heard of something called a sewing bird. This is a decorative clamp, dating back to the Victorian period, that is secured to a table edge. The 'mouth' or clamp element of the bird holds the end of the seam while you stitch from the beginning end, pulling the seam tight (**C**).

If looking for or using something like a sewing bird seems like your thing, then it is easy enough to improvise the tension it creates in other ways. For example, you can pin the end of the seam to a cushion or pillow on your lap, and then pull against that (**D**). Or, if you like to stitch at a desk or table, you will find that you can hold the end of the patches down on the table with the hand that holds the needle, creating natural tension between your hand and the table. I do something similar to this when I sit in a chair, as I rest the work on my lap, and hold the edges down with the side of my hand. You can also hold the ends of the patchwork in your needle hand, holding them between your little finger and your ring finger (**E**).

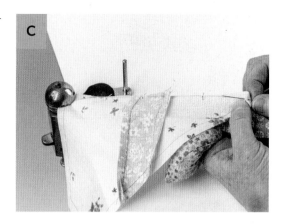

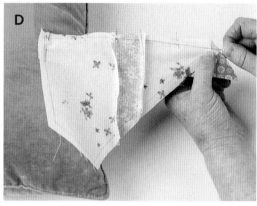

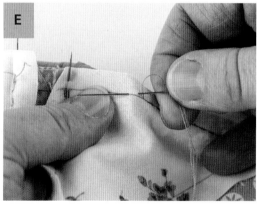

Fifties (left) and Victorian (right) sewing birds.

The sewing bird from the Fifties is actually very heavy, and the fabric is clamped within the sphere on top.

The Japanese use something similar to a sewing bird: it is a very heavy block that sits on the table, holding down your fabric. All these devices work very well for long seams such as those when sewing the borders on a quilt or joining the backing fabric.

Keeping things organized

Once fabrics are cut and I am getting ready to stitch, I like to keep the pieces for each block together. You can do this in small project bags, or use plastic bags for food storage that you can buy in the supermarket.

I use project clips frequently as I can then put all the pieces of lots of blocks in one bag for safe transportation.

Look at the Book of Blocks (see page 32) for one idea to keep sewn and partly sewn blocks flat and organized.

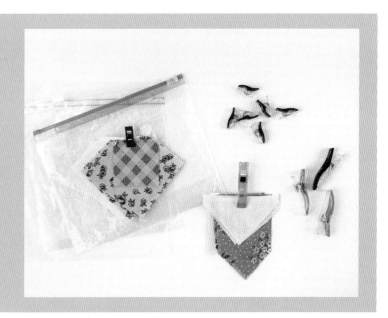

PRESSING SEAMS

Pressing seams for hand-pieced quilts is not the same as for those that are machine pieced.

Unlike machine-piecing, which requires you to press the seams as you sew, and to press in certain directions, with hand-piecing you press only when you've finished making the block. The seams also tend to fall naturally in a certain direction, so you can simply press in the angle the block dictates.

Each block has a suggested pressing, but feel free to press differently if that minimizes the bulk at the seam junctions more happily for you.

If you wish to re-press the seams, this is also possible: as the seams are not stitched down (see page 27), there is flexibility in altering their direction.

PIECING

SEWING A SINGLE SEAM

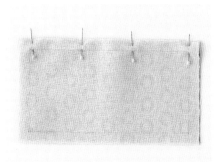

1 Pin the two patches RS together at the start and finish of the stitching line, and in between as necessary. Remember to pin on the sewing line and into the seam allowance. I tend to pin the seam line in 1in (2.5cm) increments.

2 Flip up one patch so the right sides of both patches are facing up. This will help you see what the seam will look like before you stitch it. It may not be so important on a straight seam like this, but on seams with curves or more patches it will help you see how accurate you are before you begin stitching.

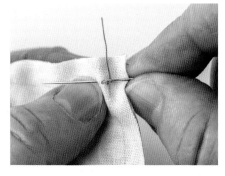

3 Thread the needle with a length of thread that tones well with the fabric and knot the end (I've deliberately used a contrasting thread for these steps). Remove the first pin and insert the needle on the corner to make the first stitch, then work a backstitch. Note: I'm right-handed, so am sewing from right to left. If you are left-handed, you will be sewing from left to right.

4 Continue along the pinned edge, making small running stitches up to the pin, then backstitch at the pin. Remove the pin then sew in the same way to the next pin. This backstitch will stop the thread gathering up if it gets pulled and will give your seam a nice, even tension.

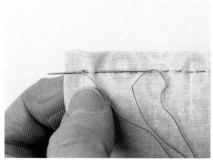

5 When you reach the end of the seam, bring the needle up from the back where the last pin is on the corner.

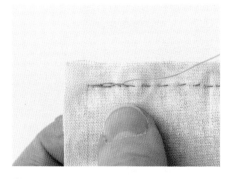

6 Make three backstitches back along your seam (so in reverse). Snip the thread, leaving a tail of about 1in (2.5cm) in length. This will give you some thread assurance if the seam gets pulled – if the thread is cut very close to the stitches, it could start to unravel.

SEWING A SEAM WITH A JUNCTION

When stitching two units together, such as those that make up the Flying Geese design (see page 42) there will likely be a junction along the joining edge (where two SAs meet). It makes it easier not to sew down the SA, in case you want to press it in a certain direction later. The pressing of the SA is something that is done when the work is finished. So, the answer is simply to skip the SAs and not sew them down.

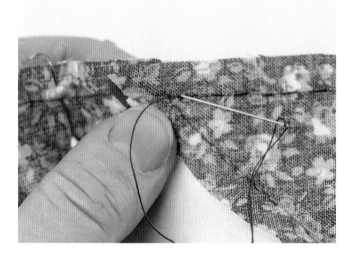

1 In this example, I am sewing together two Flying-Geese units (each unit is made up of three patches – see below). Pin your pieces as shown opposite, RS together on the seam line and into the SA.

2 Start stitching as usual from the corner and progress towards the upright SA junction. Make sure the upright SA is pushed away from the seam you are sewing so that you do not accidently sew it down (if you're right-handed it'll be towards the left; if you are left-handed, it will be towards to right).

3 When you get close to the end of the seam on the first patch, make sure that you come up at the end of the first patch seam line, ready to make a new stitch.

4 Take the needle down and underneath the SA.

5 Come up on the other side of the upright SA, ahead of the junction. Now move the upright SA towards the seam line you have just sewn. Make a backstitch at the beginning of the second patch seam line, which will start your next seam. By making this backstitch after skipping the seam, you will lock the stitches to stop them gaping at this point.

6 Continue on to the end of the seam as usual.

Joined Flying-Geese units with a skipped junction.

SEWING A SEAM WITH MATCHING JUNCTIONS

When sewing something like a Four Patch block together (see page 36), you will have SAs – one on one unit, one on the other – that match up in what will be the middle of your seam line. Just like a single junction, the best way to deal with this is to skip the SAs and not sew down either of them. The method below shows how to do this, and still leave you with a nice precise join.

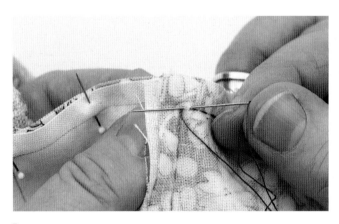

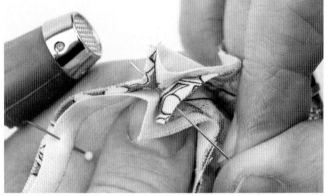

1 Pin the pair of patch units RS together along the seam line and into the SA as before. If you are right-handed, make sure that, as you approach the two seams from the right, you push them both away to the left before pinning at the end of the seam. (If you are left-handed then push to the right.) Sew along the seam, up to the junction, following the 'Sewing a single seam' instructions on page 26.

2 As you approach the seam junction, at the end of your first patch seam line, make sure that the needle will go down at the end, as though it is going into the back of the work. As you go down at the corner, push the needle through the junction at a diagonal angle, keeping the SA on the front to the left and the one on the back to the right.

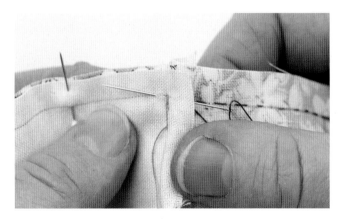

3 Take the needle up ahead of the corner on the back of the work, ready for a backstitch.

4 By making the backstitch and pulling tight, the junction will be knitted together.

5 Continue along and finish as usual.

SEWING A SEAM WITH CONVERGING JUNCTIONS

There will come a time when you'll sew some blocks that have as many as eight seams coming together at a junction (for example, Wishing Star on page 66). This is not as daunting as it sounds. By ensuring the patches are stitched together in pairs, and then those pairs stitched into two halves of the block, you'll see the approach is similar to sewing a seam with matching junctions, shown opposite.

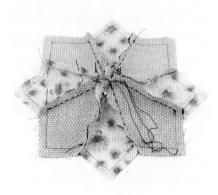 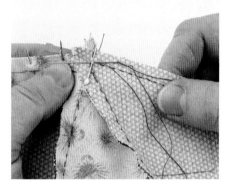 

1 Here, I am sewing together a block with eight patches. Sew the patches in pairs first, right sides together, as per the steps on page 26. Then sew two pairs together to make a row of four patches. If you have a block with six patches, sew a unit of three patches.

2 To join the two sections, begin by placing them RS together, matching the longest edges. Start stitching from one outer SA to the centre, as per the steps on page 26. When you reach the end of the seam line at the centre (indicated by the white-headed pin above), begin to make a backstitch.

3 At the end of the backstitch, take the needle diagonally through to the 'back' section and finish the backstitch, folding the SAs facing you to the left and the SAs facing away from you towards the side already stitched.

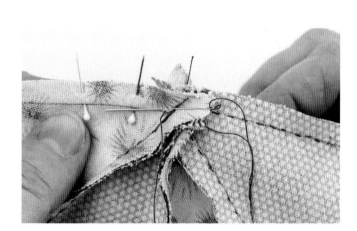 

4 Take the needle back to the 'front' section, to the left of the seam allowance (note how I have folded the SAs towards the side already stitched). Make a backstitch, then continue to sew up the left-hand side as per page 26.

Finished block with converging junctions.

SETTING IN & Y-SEAMS

Set-in seams are used to construct blocks that cannot be successfully assembled with continuous straight seams; you have to sew around a corner. This is often necessary when three (or more) pieces of fabric (that may have angles other than 90 degrees) meet at one point. The seams often form a Y-shape, hence the name 'Y-seams'. Sewing set-in seams by hand is very straightforward, and once perfected it will allow you to stitch a wider variety of blocks. The Bow Tie block shown here (see also page 50) is a good example to start with, but you will also be using this method on other blocks such as Bright Hopes (see page 46).

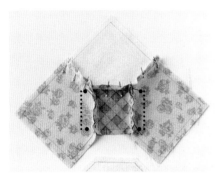

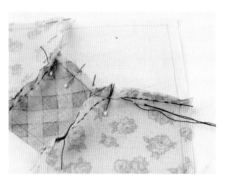

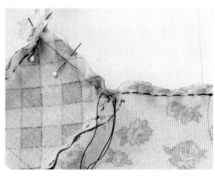

1 Begin by sewing together the patches with straight edges, with RS facing and using the technique described on page 26. For my block, this is the square and the straight edges of the two pentagonal patches – see the dotted lines above. Once the straight edges are sewn, pin the next Y-seam patch to your joined patches, RS together.

2 Start stitching from one outer SA towards the end of the inner SA, as detailed in the steps on page 26. Begin to make a backstitch.

3 At the end of the backstitch, take the needle behind the SA then through to the next patch. Note how the SA facing you is pushed towards the newly stitched seam, once the needle is in the next patch. Make a backstitch.

4 Stitch along the next edge as described on page 26: start to make a backstitch, then take the needle through to the next patch (behind the SA) to finish the backstitch. Make a backstitch then work the next edge. Sew in the same way described on page 26.

Set in Y-seam.
The final patch is added in exactly the same way.

ROUND PIECES & CURVED SEAMS

With some preparation and considered sewing, curved seams and round pieces are much easier to sew than many quilters believe – especially if you are hand sewing your patches together. I like to use the pinning method described here, as I find this creates the neatest finish.

1 I like to work by pinning the concave curve to the convex curve. I find this works best for me as I can see the excess fabric that I'm easing round the curve and can hold it in place with pins. With RS facing, begin by pinning the curved edges of the patches with three pins – one in the centre and one at each end of the seam. Make sure that the ends of the patches align.

2 Once you're happy with how the fabric is lying with the three pins, add more pins in between – the number will vary depending on the size of your unit or block.

3 Simply sew the curved seam following the technique on page 26. As we have more pins and they are sitting closer to each other, I like to backstitch every ½in (1.25cm).

BOOK OF **BLOCKS**

Having somewhere to store your blocks as you stitch them is always a good idea. A large flat storage box is handy, but if you are out and about with your work for group sewing, or stitching on the go, then a cumbersome box might not be the most practical.

Here is a solution for rolling and storing the blocks – it's quick and easy to make, and you may be able to use materials and notions you already have to hand.

Finished size

20in (50.75cm) tall; 3¾in (9.5cm) wide when rolled up empty, and 26in (66cm) wide unrolled

You will need

For the book's cover:

▸ 1yd (1m) of ½in (1.25cm) wide tape or ribbon

▸ One button, approx. ¾in (2cm) in diameter

▸ One tea towel, approx. 18½ x 28in (47 x 71.25cm)

OR

20 x 30in (50.75 x 76.25cm) of heavyweight cotton or similar, such as Essex Linen – this will give the book some body

Use any or all of the following for your pages:

▸ 18 x 26in (45.75 x 66cm) of cotton wadding/batting

▸ 18 x 26in (45.75 x 66cm) felt piece

▸ Several 18 x 26in (45.75 x 66cm) flannel-backed tablecloth pieces – these allow the patches to stick to the flannel, but the smooth side means the patches don't stick to other pages

▸ 18 x 26in (48.25 x 66cm) of gridded design wall fabric

METHOD

1 The edges of the pages may need to be neatened before inserting into your book. You can do this by folding a narrow hem (about ¼in or 5mm deep), by binding the edges (see page 122), or simply finishing them with zigzag stitch or overlock/serger stitch. Whichever you choose, just neaten three sides – two long edges and one short edge. The remaining short edge will be concealed in the bound edge of the book roll. Any of the page types will be useful to lay pieces of your blocks on as you design and sew them. The patches can be pinned in place for transportation, but mostly the cotton pieces will stick to the wadding/batting or design wall fabric. Choose as many or as few page types as you like.

2 If you are using yardage for your book's cover, instead of a tea towel, turn over the edges on all four sides to stitch a double hem and neaten the raw edges.

3 Find the middle of one of the short sides of the book's cover and mark on the RS. Fold the tape or ribbon in half and pin the fold of the tape or ribbon over the halfway point.

4 Place the button on top of the tape or ribbon centre and stitch in place through the ribbon or tape and the book-cover piece.

5 Place the pages on the WS of the book piece, 2in (5cm) in from the (short) left-hand side (the side without the ribbon and button). The unbound or unfinished edge of each page should run parallel to the left-hand edge of the book-cover piece.

6 Fold over the left-hand edge of the book-cover piece to the right, over and onto the pages therefore enclosing the pages' raw edges. Pin.

7 Machine stitch through all the layers then sew a second line ½in (1.25cm) from the folded edge.

8 The book is now ready for you to put your blocks inside, ready for working on when you are out and about. To tie the book closed, simply roll the book loosely from the bound end and secure with the tape or ribbon in a bow.

THE **BLOCKS**

1

TWO PATCH
& FOUR PATCH

Squares are probably the simplest units to stitch together, offering many design options depending on fabric choice and colour placement. In the sampler quilt (see page 94), I've used the Two Patch blocks as a border round the Arrowhead Block (see page 72 for the block, and page 101 for the joined blocks).

METHOD

1 Stitch the squares together in pairs to make a Two Patch block.

2 To make a Four Patch block, stitch two Two Patch blocks together.

3 Press.

 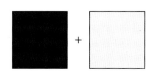

 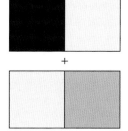

Making the sampler quilt

I made twenty-eight Two Patch blocks for my quilt (see page 94). If you'd like to do this, you will need to multiply the cutting amounts for the Two Patch by 28.

Finished sizes
Two Patch: 2 x 4in (5 x 10cm)
Four Patch: 4in (10cm) square

Cut
Two Patch:
▶ one light-coloured A piece
▶ one medium-/ dark-coloured A piece

Four Patch:
▶ two light-coloured A pieces
▶ two medium-/ dark-coloured A pieces
(these can be the same colour or contrasting colours)

Templates
Shown smaller here and in colour for reference. For actual-size templates, see page 130.

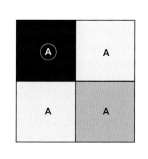

**FOUR PATCH BLOCK
FROM THE FRONT:**

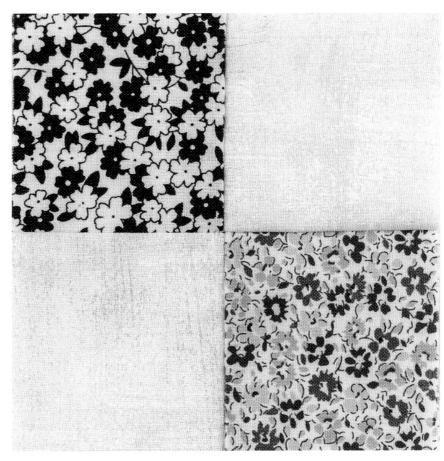

**FOUR PATCH BLOCK BLOCK
FROM THE BACK, PRESSED:**

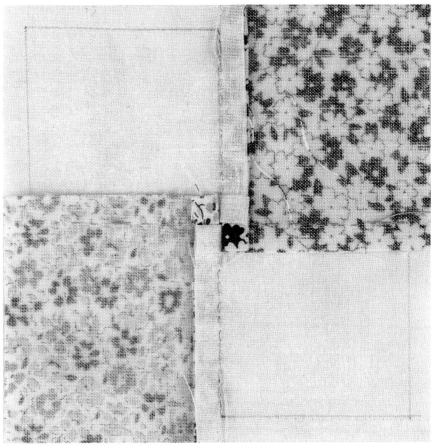

2

HALF SQUARE TRIANGLE

The Half Square Triangle (HST) is a simple design that offers many possibilities. In the sampler quilt, I've stitched four units together in a design known as Broken Dishes (see below), but many more options are possible; see the variations at the bottom of this page.

METHOD

1 Stitch two HSTs together along the bias (long diagonal) edge. Be careful not to stretch the edge you are stitching, as this has more give in it than the other two sides of the triangle.

2 Press.

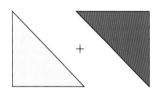

VARIATIONS

Broken Dishes

Pinwheel

Mock Flying Geese

Simple chevrons

Finished size
3in (7.5cm) square

Cut
▸ one light-coloured A piece
▸ one medium-/ dark-coloured A piece

Templates
Shown smaller here and in colour for reference.
For actual-size templates, see page 131.

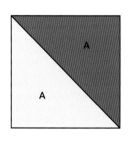

Making the sampler quilt
I made twenty HST blocks for my quilt (see page 94). If you'd like to do this, you will need to multiply the cutting amounts by 20.

BLOCK FROM THE FRONT:

BLOCK FROM THE BACK, PRESSED:

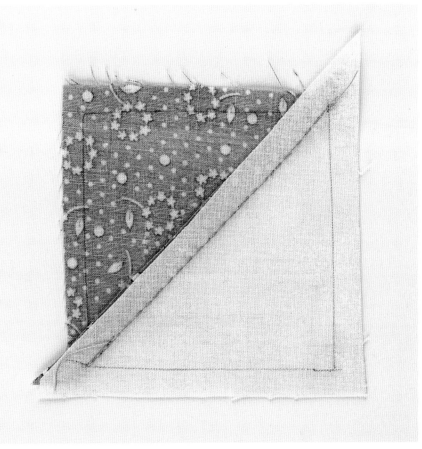

KANSAS DUGOUT

This is a simple block when it is used on its own, but the design presents you with lots of possibilities when you start to play with the layout of multiple blocks. For example, you could swap the light and dark fabrics to give the block a different look.

METHOD

1 Stitch triangles B to either side of piece A. Take care when sewing: these seams are stretchy as they are cut on the bias of the fabric.

2 Press.

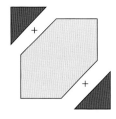

Finished size

3in (7.5cm) square

Cut

▶ one light-coloured A piece

▶ two medium-/ dark-coloured B pieces

Templates

Shown smaller here and in colour for reference.
For actual-size templates, see page 131.

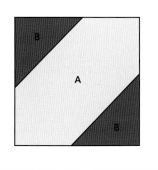

Making the sampler quilt

I made eleven Kansas Dugout blocks for my quilt (see page 94). If you'd like to do this, you will need to multiply the cutting amounts by 11.

BLOCK FROM THE FRONT:

BLOCK FROM THE BACK, PRESSED:

4

FLYING GEESE

This is a simple block consisting of two different sizes of triangle, and its name references the flight of geese in the sky. Old quilts can be seen with rows of these all flying in the same direction and then one row quirkily going the other way. Below shows the easiest method if you're new to patchwork. If you have more experience, you could sew the two A triangles in one continuous line of stitching, as you start at the base with both methods.

Finished size
3 x 6in (7.5 x 15.25cm)

Cut
▸ two medium-/dark-coloured A pieces
▸ one light-coloured B piece

Templates
Shown smaller here and in colour for reference.
For actual-size templates,
see pages 130 and 131.

METHOD

1 Stitch one triangle A to one side of triangle B. Take care as the seams are on the bias and so may stretch.

2 Repeat with the remaining triangle A on the opposite side of triangle B.

3 Press.

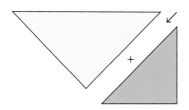

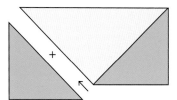

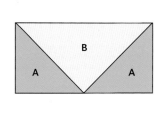

Making the sampler quilt

I made five Flying Geese blocks for my quilt (see page 94). If you'd like to do this, you will need to multiply the cutting amounts by 5.

BLOCK FROM THE FRONT:

BLOCK FROM THE BACK, PRESSED:

5

ALBUM

Originally named the Snowflake block back in 1897, this block was renamed Maud's Album Quilt some time in the 1930s. The light-coloured patches would be inscribed with the names of family and friends, so they could be remembered when the quilt was in use.

METHOD

1 Stitch A pieces to either side of a B piece. Make two.

2 Stitch B pieces to either side of the C piece.

3 Stitch the three sections together.

4 Press.

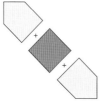

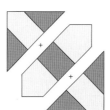

Finished size

6in (15.25cm) square

Cut

Option 1:

▶ four medium-/dark-coloured A pieces

▶ four light-coloured B pieces

▶ one medium-/dark-coloured C piece

Option 2:

▶ four light-coloured A pieces

▶ four medium-/dark-coloured B pieces

▶ one light-coloured C piece

Templates

Shown smaller here and in colour for reference.
For actual-size templates, see pages 130 and 131.

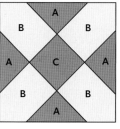

Option 1

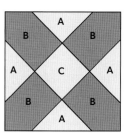

Option 2

Making the sampler quilt

For my quilt (see page 94), I made two Album blocks in the option 1 colourway, and three blocks in the option 2 colourway. If you'd like to do this, you will need to multiply the cutting amounts for option 1 by 2, and option 2 by 3.

BLOCK FROM THE FRONT:

BLOCK FROM THE BACK, PRESSED:

6

BRIGHT HOPES

This is a simple block of rectangles around a square, first published in 1945. It may represent a window, with the name perhaps coming from the bright hope of looking through to the daylight. However, as with many quilt-block names, we can only speculate and imagine what inspired the maker. Note that, depending on which way you start to stitch, the block will rotate in different directions.

Finished size

6in (15.25cm) square

Cut

▸ one light-coloured A piece

▸ four medium-/dark-coloured B pieces, two in one colour and two in another

Templates

Shown smaller here and in colour for reference.
For actual-size templates, see pages 130 and 131.

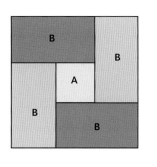

METHOD

1 Stitch the A piece to a B piece. You will only be stitching the length of A.

2 Now stitch a second B to the right-hand side of the joined patches.

3 Continue with the third B.

4 Join a fourth B piece. The seam will be a set-in seam to allow you to stitch round a corner (see page 30).

5 Press.

VARIATION

Making the sampler quilt

I made five Bright Hopes blocks for my quilt (see page 94). If you'd like to do this, you will need to multiply the cutting amounts by 5.

1

2

3

4

BLOCK FROM THE FRONT:

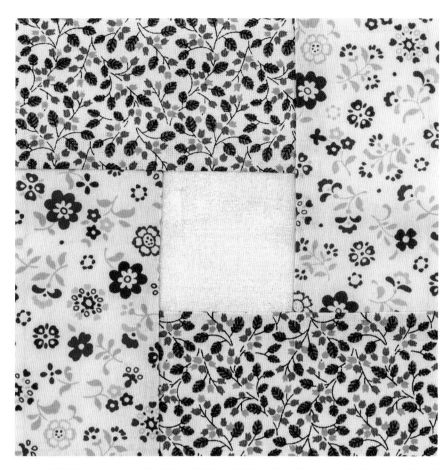

BLOCK FROM THE BACK, PRESSED:

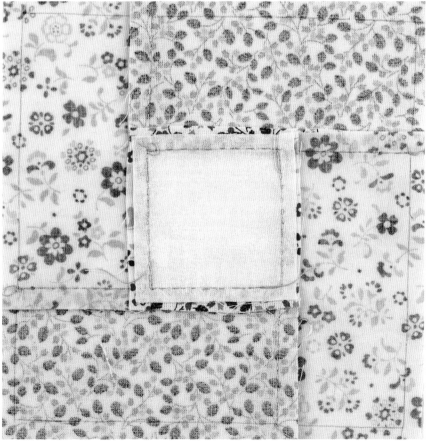

7

SPOOLS

You can have some fun with this representational block of an empty thread spool. Try using a striped fabric to represent thread around the spool, or just make the spool in one fabric to make it empty.

METHOD

1 Stitch the medium-/dark-coloured B pieces to either side of the A piece.

2 Stitch the light-coloured B pieces to the remaining sides of the A piece, setting them in as you stitch.

3 Press.

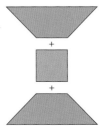

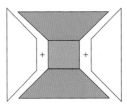

Finished size
6in (15.25cm) square

Cut

▶ one medium-/dark-coloured A piece

▶ two light-coloured B pieces

▶ two medium-/dark-coloured B pieces

Templates
Shown smaller here and in colour for reference.
For actual-size templates, see pages 130 and 131.

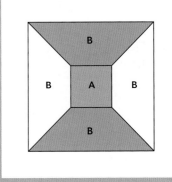

Making the sampler quilt

I made five Spool blocks for my quilt (see page 94), two in one colourway and three in three other colourways. If you'd like to do this, you will need to multiply the cutting amounts by 5 to make one colourway, or by 2 in colourway 1 then by 1 for the remaining three colourways.

BLOCK FROM THE FRONT:

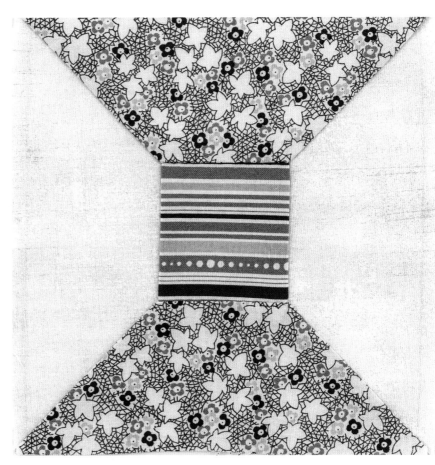

BLOCK FROM THE BACK, PRESSED:

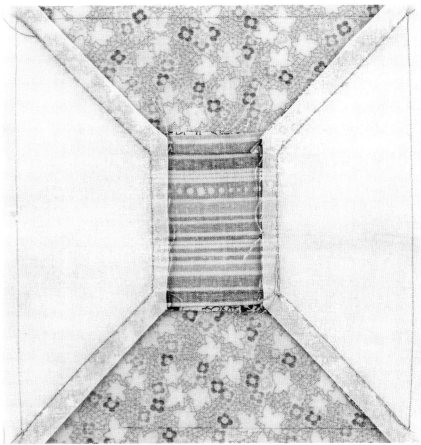

8

BOW TIE

This block name was coined in the 1930s and has varied very little over the decades. I often think it would be fun to make a quilt of these using old shirts and actual tie fabrics. I've used a check fabric as the middle of the block here to represent the knotting of the tie, but use whatever fabrics have meaning for you, or look good together. Refer also to the setting-in technique on page 30.

Refer also to the setting-in technique on page 30.

Finished size
6in (15.25cm) square

Cut
▶ one medium-/dark-coloured A piece
▶ two light-coloured B pieces
▶ two medium-/dark-coloured B pieces

Templates
Shown smaller here and in colour for reference.
For actual-size templates, see page 130.

For actual-size templates, see page 130.

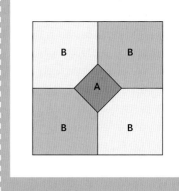

METHOD

1 Stitch a medium-/dark coloured B piece to either side of the A piece.

2 Stitch the light-coloured B pieces to the remaining sides of the A piece, setting them in as you stitch.

3 Press.

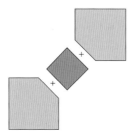

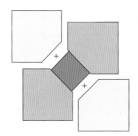

Making the sampler quilt

I made five Bow Tie blocks for my quilt (see page 94). If you'd like to do this, you will need to multiply the cutting amounts by 5.

(see page 94)

BLOCK FROM THE FRONT:

BLOCK FROM THE BACK, PRESSED:

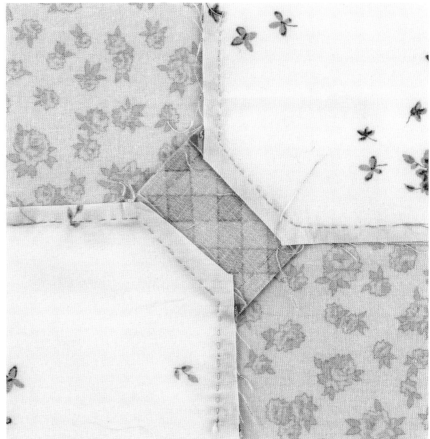

9

SNOWBALL

Snowball is one of my favourite curved blocks. It has lots of colour-placement combinations, all giving the basic block units different names. The gentle curves on this will ease you in gently to curved piecing. Refer also to the technique on page 31.

Finished size

6in (15.25cm) square

Cut

▸ two medium/dark-coloured B pieces

▸ one light-coloured A piece

Templates

Shown smaller here and in colour for reference.
For actual-size templates, see page 132.

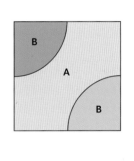

METHOD

1 Stitch the B pieces to either side of the A piece.

2 Press.

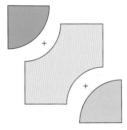

Making the sampler quilt

I made five Snowball blocks for my quilt (see page 94), two in one colourway and three in another. If you'd like to do this, you will need to multiply the cutting amounts by 5 to make one colourway, or by 2 in colourway 1 then by 3 in colourway 2.

BLOCK FROM THE FRONT:

BLOCK FROM THE BACK, PRESSED:

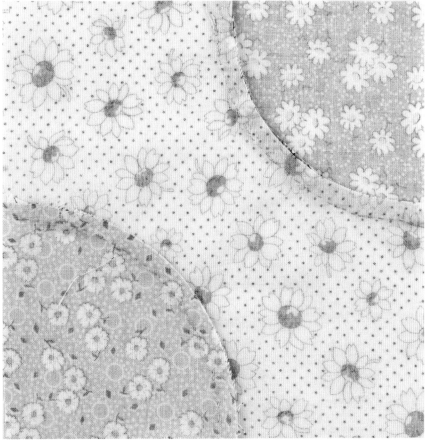

10

MILL & STAR

Four of these blocks set together create the mill wheel in the centre, but on their own make an eye-catching design, as with many patchwork blocks in this book. This is a nice block to use up little scraps, and you could even fussy cut for the stars.

METHOD

1 Stitch a light-coloured B piece to one side of an A piece. Stitch a BR piece to the other side of the A piece.

2 Repeat step 1 to make two light-coloured sections in total.

3 Repeat steps 1 and 2 to make two medium-coloured sections in total.

4 Stitch a light section to a medium section. Repeat.

5 Stitch the two sections together.

6 Press.

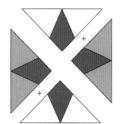

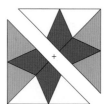

Finished size

6in (15.25cm) square

Cut

- ▸ four dark-coloured A pieces
  - ▸ two medium-coloured BR pieces
  - ▸ two medium-coloured B pieces
    - ▸ two light-coloured BR pieces
    - ▸ two light-coloured B pieces

Templates

Shown smaller here and in colour for reference.
For actual-size templates, see page 132.

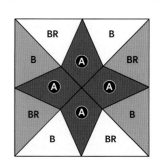

Making the sampler quilt

I made five Mill & Star blocks for my quilt (see page 94), two in colourway 1, two in colourway 2 and one in colourway 3. If you'd like to do this, you will need to multiply the cutting amounts by 5 to make them in one colourway, or by the following amounts for various colourway:

– by 2 in colourway 1

– by 2 in colourway 2

– by 1 in colourway 3.

BLOCK FROM THE FRONT:

BLOCK FROM THE BACK, PRESSED:

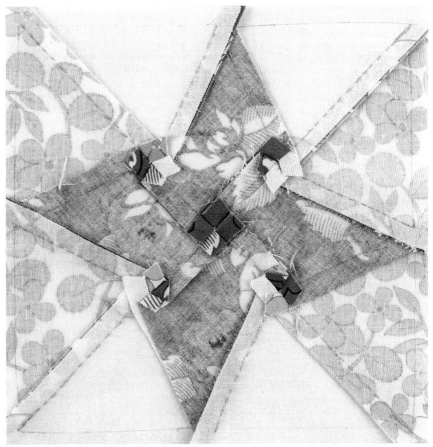

11

COURTHOUSE STEPS

This is a lovely setting for blocks as it gives them a multi-layered frame. Smaller plain squares are often used for the centre, but this block works well as a frame to make a small block a bigger size. You can adapt Courthouse Steps to fit any size block – simply start with strips that are the same height as your block, then increase the lengths of each pair strips by 2in (5cm) as you work outwards. For my quilt, I used it around the Wishing Star block (see page 66).

METHOD

Note: All the strips are pressed away from the centre block.

1 Stitch the 10in (25.5cm) light-coloured strips to the left and right edges of the central block.

2 Stitch the 12in (30.5cm) dark-coloured strips to the top and bottom edges of the central block.

3 Stitch the 12in (30.5cm) light-coloured strips to left and right edges of the block.

4 Repeat in this way, adding strips that increase in length with each 'round', until the strips are used up.

5 Press.

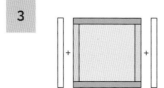

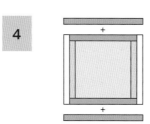

Finished size

Sample is 18in (45.75cm) square, using 1in (2.5cm) wide strips

Cut

From dark-coloured fabric:
- two 12 x 1in (30.5 x 2.5cm) pieces
- two 14 x 1in (35.5 x 2.5cm) pieces
- two 16 x 1in (40.75 x 2.5cm) pieces
- two 18 x 1in (45.75 x 2.5cm) pieces

From light-coloured fabric:
- two 10 x 1in (25.5 x 2.5cm) pieces
- two 12 x 1in (30.5 x 2.5cm) pieces
- two 14 x 1in (35.5 x 2.5cm) pieces
- two 16 x 1in (40.75 x 2.5cm) pieces

Templates

Shown smaller here and in colour for reference.
For actual-size templates, see page 132.

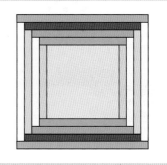

Making the sampler quilt

I made one Courthouse Steps block for my quilt (see page 94).

12

WOVEN RIBBONS

One of the vintage quilts that I saw when I was researching for this book contained a version of this block. This self-drafted version looks great with four contrasting fabrics to emphasize the woven effect.

Finished size

12in (30.5cm) square

Cut

▸ **Background/light:**
  one E, four B, four A
▸ **Colour 1 (blue floral):**
  one C, one D
▸ **Colour 2 (blue cross):**
  one C, one D
▸ **Colour 3 (red floral):**
  one C, one D
▸ **Colour 4 (red dots):**
  one C, one D

Templates

Shown smaller here and in colour
for reference.
For actual-size templates,
see pages 131 and 133.

1

METHOD

Note: Before stitching the pieces together, I recommend arranging them in front of you to make sure you place the right colours in the right sections/units.

1 Stitch pieces A, B and D together, then add C. Pieces C and D should be different colours. Repeat with the remaining pieces to make four units in total.

2 Stitch piece E to one unit.

3 Sew a unit to the section with piece E.

4 Add the remaining units.

5 Press.

2

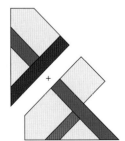

Making the sampler quilt

I made one Woven Ribbon block for my quilt (see page 94).

3

4

BLOCK FROM THE FRONT:

BLOCK FROM THE BACK, PRESSED:

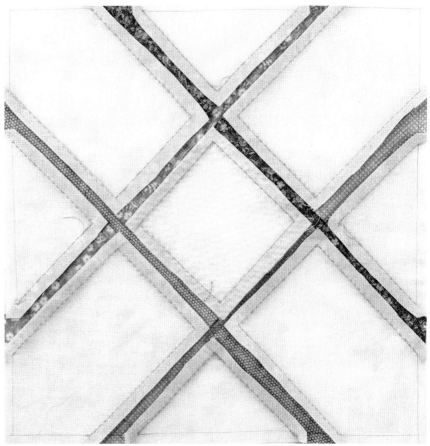

PANSY

It's always amazing when simple fabric shapes are transformed into a recognizable pattern by careful colour selection. I love how the sashing on two sides of each block, which I've done on the final quilt, gives this block a real garden-path feeling (see page 98).

METHOD

1 Sew two petals (C pieces) together. Repeat to make two pairs in total.

2 With one pair, set in the centre (A piece in colour 1).

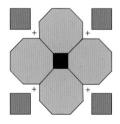

3 Add the remaining pair of petals to the pair with the centre, setting them in (see page 30 for the technique).

4 Set in four leaves (A pieces in colour 3) around the petals.

5 Stitch two background B pieces together in pairs. Repeat to make four pairs in total. These are the corner pieces.

6 Set in the corners around the petals.

7 Press.

8 I added sashing strips around the Pansy block for my final quilt. See page 90 for more information about adding sashing.

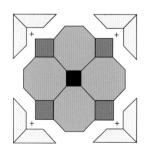

13

Finished size

7in (17.75cm) square

Cut

▸ **Background/light:**
  eight B pieces

▸ **Colour 1 (centre):**
  one A piece

▸ **Colour 2 (petals):**
  four C pieces

▸ **Colour 3 (leaves):**
  four A pieces

Templates

Shown smaller here and in colour for reference.
For actual-size templates, for both the block and its sashing, see page 134.

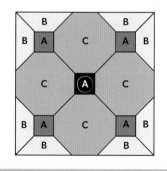

Making the sampler quilt

I made four Pansy blocks for my quilt (see page 94), two in one colourway and two in another. If you'd like to do this, you will need to multiply the cutting amounts by 4 to make one colourway, or by 2 in colourway 1 then by 2 in colourway 2.

BLOCK FROM THE FRONT:

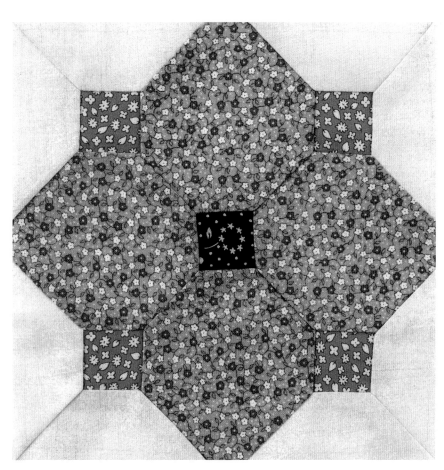

BLOCK FROM THE BACK, PRESSED:

14

GRANDMOTHER'S STAR

Hexagons are a popular shape in patchwork, and it's nice to be able to incorporate them into a quilt of square blocks. The classic Grandmother's flower garden rosette sits nicely here with the 'leaves' poking out and a clever infill, creating a square.

Finished size

12in (30.5cm) square

Cut

From background/ light-coloured fabric:

▶ two CR pieces

▶ two D pieces

▶ two C pieces

Colour 1:

▶ one A piece (centre)

Colour 2:

▶ three A pieces

Colour 3:

▶ three A pieces

Colour 4:

▶ six B pieces

Templates

Shown smaller here and in colour for reference.
For actual-size templates, see page 135.

METHOD

1 Stitch an A piece in colour 2 to the top of the A piece in colour 1. Stitch an A piece in colour 3 to the bottom of the A piece in colour 1.

2 Stitch the remaining A pieces together in pairs, sewing colour 2 to colour 3. Then, stitch the pairs either side of the A unit with three pieces, setting them in.

3 Set in the B pieces.

4 Set in the D pieces.

5 Set in the C and CR pieces.

6 Press.

1
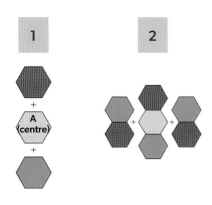

2
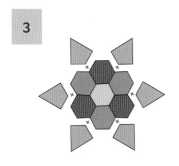

3

4
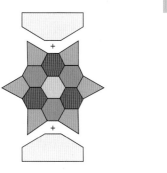

5
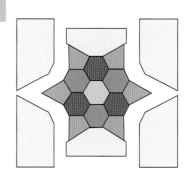

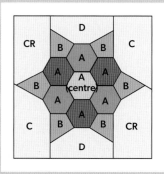

Making the sampler quilt

I made one Grandmother's Star block for my quilt (see page 94).

BLOCK FROM THE FRONT:

BLOCK FROM THE BACK, PRESSED:

15

WESTERN STAR

I love the star within a star design here. You can emphasize the central star by using the same coloured fabrics for pieces A and B, or keep it clean and simple by using the same fabric as pieces D and E. Like so many of the blocks in this sampler quilt, perhaps a whole quilt of your favourite block is calling to be stitched?

METHOD

1 Stitch all the B pieces around the A piece.

2 Set in the C pieces.

3 Set in the D and E pieces, starting with the D pieces.

4 Press.

1

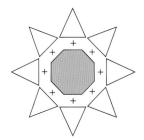

2

3

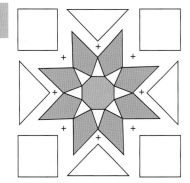

Finished size

12in (30.5cm) square

Cut

**From background/
light-coloured fabric:**

▸ four E pieces

▸ four D pieces

▸ eight B pieces

**From medium-/
dark-coloured fabric:**

▸ one A piece

▸ eight C pieces

Templates

Shown smaller here and in colour for reference.
For actual-size templates, see pages 134 and 135.

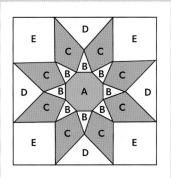

Making the sampler quilt

I made one Western Star block for my quilt (see page 94).

BLOCK FROM THE FRONT:

BLOCK FROM THE BACK, PRESSED:

16

WISHING STAR

This is fun star block that, depending on the colour placement for pieces A and B, will give the effect of a square and a square on point. If fussy cutting is something you like doing, then this block can give you lots of opportunities for that – either for the centre of the star, or the main star points.

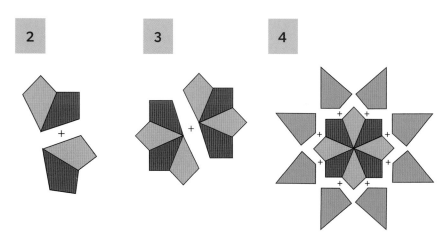

METHOD

1 Stitch an A piece to a B piece. Make four pairs in total. Note the balance marks; these help when adding the C and CR pieces. Mark these in, within the SA.

2 Stitch two A+B pairs together. Repeat with the remaining pairs.

3 Stitch the two A+B sections together.

4 Set in the C and CR pieces, taking note of the balance marks and matching up accordingly.

5 Set in the D and E pieces, staring with the D pieces.

6 Press.

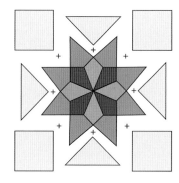

Finished size
10in (25.5cm) square

Cut
From background/ light-coloured fabric:
▶ four D pieces
▶ four E pieces

From medium-/ dark-coloured fabric:
▶ four A pieces
▶ four B pieces
▶ four C pieces
▶ four CR pieces

Templates
Shown smaller here for reference. For actual-size templates, see pages 131 and 144.

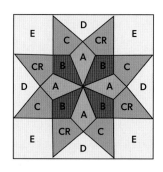

Making the sampler quilt
I made one Wishing Star block for my quilt (see page 94).

BLOCK FROM THE FRONT:

BLOCK FROM THE BACK, PRESSED:

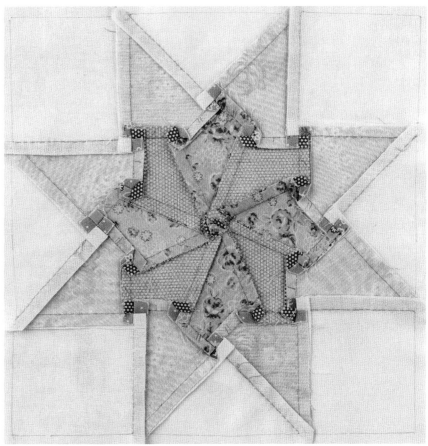

DRUSILLA'S DELIGHT

17

As with all the blocks in this book, for Drusilla's Delight I've stayed true to the original name found in reference books on patchwork blocks. Some block names, like this one, seem quite personal – was this block really named for a person? Either way, it's a fun block to stitch and you could experiment with some striped fabric for pieces A, D and DR, depending on your fabric stash.

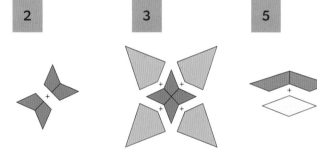

METHOD

1 Stitch the A pieces together in pairs.

2 Stitch the A-piece pairs together.

3 Set in the B pieces.

4 Stitch a D piece to a DR piece. Make four in total.

5 Stitch a D+DR section to a C piece. Make four in total.

6 Stitch an E piece to an ER piece. Make four in total.

7 Set in the D+DR + C units to the A+B unit.

8 Set in the corner E+ER units around the block.

9 Press.

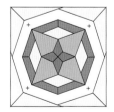

Finished size
12in (30.5cm) square

Cut
From background/ light-coloured fabric:
▸ four E pieces
▸ four ER pieces
▸ four C pieces

From medium-/ dark-coloured fabric:
▸ four A pieces
▸ four B pieces
▸ four D pieces
▸ four DR pieces

Templates
Shown smaller here and in colour for reference.
For actual-size templates, see page 136.

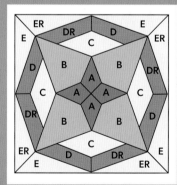

Making the sampler quilt
I made one Drusilla's Delight block for my quilt (see page 94).

BLOCK FROM THE FRONT:

BLOCK FROM THE BACK, PRESSED:

18

SOUTHERN STAR

Using a stripe or a fussy-cut motif for the centre (A and AR) pieces here will give a lovely kaleidoscopic effect; for my sampler quilt I broke up the design with two contrasting prints (see page 94). Using a lighter print, or the same background fabric for pieces B and BR isolates the central design and allows the star points to radiate. There are lots of pieces in this block, so take the time to lay them out first.

METHOD

1 Stitch an A piece to an AR piece. Make four pairs in total. Note the balance marks; mark these in, within the SA, before sewing the A and AR pieces together. These marks will help with accurate placement.

2 Stitch two pairs together. Repeat with the remaining pairs.

3 Stitch the two A+AR sections together.

4 Stitch a B piece and a BR piece to a C piece. Make four in total.

5 Stitch these around the central A+AR unit.

6 Stitch an E piece and an ER piece to either side of a D piece. Make four in total.

7 Set these units around the centre of the block.

8 Press.

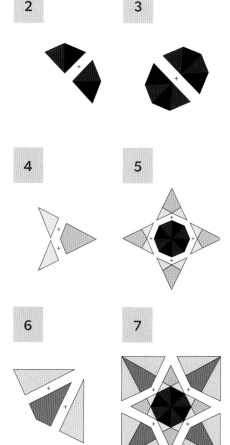

Finished size

12in (30.5cm) square

Cut

From background/ light-coloured fabric:
▸ four E pieces
▸ four ER pieces
▸ four B pieces
▸ four BR pieces

From medium-/ dark-coloured fabric:
▸ four D pieces
▸ four C pieces
▸ four A pieces
▸ four AR pieces

Templates

Shown smaller here and in colour for reference.
For actual-size templates, see pages 136 and 137.

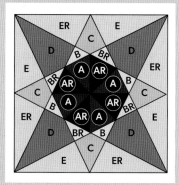

Making the sampler quilt

I made one Southern Star block for my quilt (see page 94).

BLOCK FROM THE FRONT:

BLOCK FROM THE BACK, PRESSED:

19

ARROWHEAD

This is another lovely block to make use of your scraps, and you can highlight your favourite fabric in the centre. You could use the same fabric for the centre and the first stitched pairs of pieces B and BR for a dramatic effect. Be careful when stitching this block to ensure the correct sides of the diamonds are sewn together.

METHOD

1 Stitch a B piece and a BR piece – both in colour 1 – together. Note the balance marks for the long and short sides; mark these within the SA to help with accurate piecing. Repeat to make four pairs in total.

2 Stitch a B piece in colour 2 to the BR side of a colour 1 pair, and a BR piece in colour 2 to the B side of the same pair. Again note and mark in the balance marks. Repeat, using up all the B and BR pieces in colour 2.

3 Stitch two of these units to opposite sides of the A piece.

4 Set the two remaining B+BR units into the remaining two sides of A.

5 Set in the C and D pieces, starting with the C pieces.

6 Press.

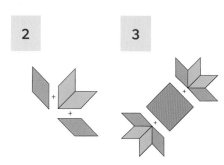
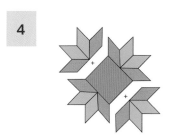

Finished size
10in (25.5cm) square

Cut
From background/ light-coloured fabric:
- four D pieces
- eight C pieces

From medium-/ dark-coloured fabric:
- eight B pieces, four in colour 1 and four in colour 2
- eight BR pieces, four in colour 1 and four in colour 2
- one A piece

Templates
Shown smaller here and in colour for reference.
For actual-size templates, see page 137.

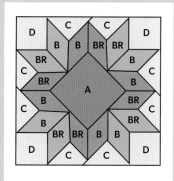

Making the sampler quilt
I made one Arrowhead block for my quilt (see page 94).

BLOCK FROM THE FRONT:

BLOCK FROM THE BACK, PRESSED:

20

CARPENTER'S WHEEL

This is a great block to stitch and it makes a real impact in a quilt, so it will be worth all the effort when piecing together. To simplify your fabric choice, you could choose two prints: one for the central star and a second for the surround.

METHOD

1 For the centre star, stitch an A piece in colour 1 to an A piece in colour 2, rotating one A piece appropriately. Repeat to make four pairs in total.

2 Stitch two A pairs together, alternating the colours. Make two in total.

3 Stitch the two halves together.

4 Set in eight B pieces around the centre star.

5 Stitch three A pieces together, one of each colour. Repeat to make eight A-piece trios, making sure to keep the colours in the same order.

6 Set these in around the centre star.

7 Set in the background B and C pieces, starting with the inner B pieces and the C pieces.

8 Press.

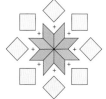

Finished size
18in (45.75cm) square

Cut
**Background pieces
(light-coloured fabric):**

- twenty B pieces
- eight C pieces

**Centre star (medium-/
dark-coloured fabric):**

- four A pieces in colour 1
- four A pieces in colour 2

**Outer ring (medium-/
dark-coloured fabric):**

- eight A pieces in colour 1
- eight A pieces in colour 2
- eight A pieces in colour 3

Templates
Shown smaller here and in colour for reference.
For actual-size templates, see pages 133 and 138.

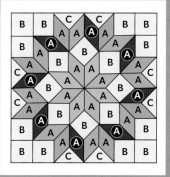

Making the sampler quilt
I made one Carpenter's Wheel block for my quilt (see page 94).

BLOCK FROM THE FRONT:

BLOCK FROM THE BACK, PRESSED:

21

MARBLES

Marbles is a great block with which to perfect your curved piecing. Lots of colourful scraps will re-create this block's namesake, but if you stick to red and white fabrics the result is reminiscent of the peppermint candy sweets seen at Christmas! To begin, ensure that you pin well along the curves. Start at each end and work towards the centre of the seam.

Note that if your template for piece B is flipped the other way when you cut it, the design will swirl in the opposite direction.

METHOD

1 Stitch a B piece in colour 1 to a B piece in colour 2. Repeat to make four pairs.

2 Stitch two pairs together. Repeat with the remaining pairs.

3 Stitch the two sections together.

4 Stitch two A pieces together to make one half of the 'frame'. Repeat with the remaining A pieces.

5 Stitch the two A 'frame' sections together.

6 Set the circle within the frame, pinning at each quarter and finger pressing at the eighth points, and matching the seams to fit and balance the pieces correctly (see page 31).

7 Press.

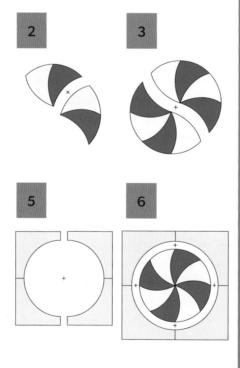

Finished size
12in (30.5cm) square

Cut
From background/ light-coloured fabric:

▸ four A pieces

From medium-/ dark-coloured fabric:

▸ eight B pieces, four in colour 1 and four in colour 2

Templates
Shown smaller here and in colour for reference.
For actual-size templates, see page 138.

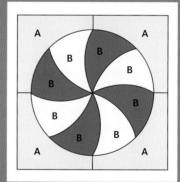

Making the quilt
I made one Marble block for my quilt (see page 94).

BLOCK FROM THE FRONT:

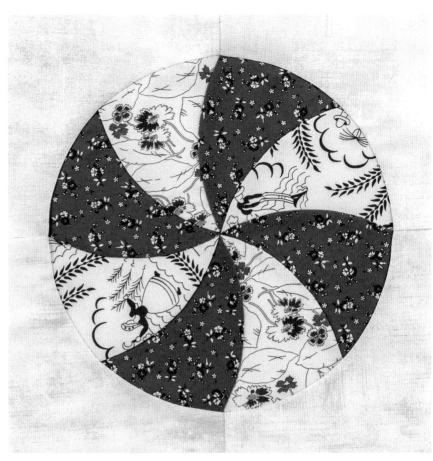

BLOCK FROM THE BACK, PRESSED:

22

WATER WHEEL

The pieced segments of the inner and outer circles really do bring the water wheel image to life, and the overall effect is worth the effort. That said, the gentle curves in this block are easier to piece than you may think. Using different prints for the inner and outer wheel gives the block a little more dimension but, equally, cutting up one large print would give enough variation in the block too.

METHOD

1 Alternating the colours, stitch the A pieces to the B pieces. Make eight units in total, four in one colour scheme and four in another colour scheme.

2 Stitch two of the units together, pairing alternate colour schemes. Repeat with the remaining units to make four quarter shapes.

3 Stitch the four quarters into two semi-circles.

4 Stitch the semi-circles together.

5 Stitch two C pieces together to make one half of the 'frame'. Repeat with the remaining C pieces.

6 Stitch the two C 'frame' halves together.

7 Set the circle within the frame, pinning at each quarter and finger pressing at the eighth points, and matching the seams on the circle to fit and balance the pieces correctly (see page 31).

8 Press.

2

3

4

6

Finished size
12in (30.5cm) square

Cut
From background/ light-coloured fabric:
▸ four C pieces

From medium-/ dark-coloured fabric:
▸ eight B pieces, four in colour 1 and four in colour 2
▸ eight A pieces, four in colour 1 and four in colour 2

Templates
Shown smaller here and in colour for reference.
For actual-size templates, see page 139.

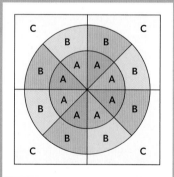

Making the sampler quilt
I made one Water Wheel block for my quilt (see page 94).

BLOCK FROM THE FRONT:

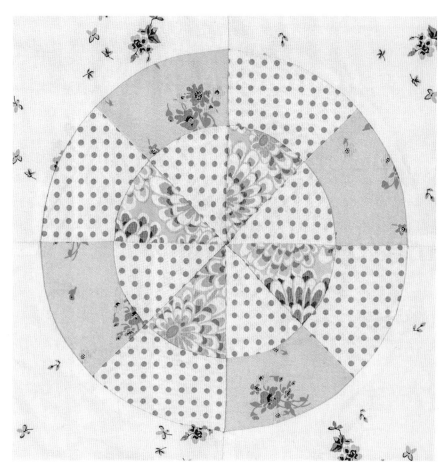

BLOCK FROM THE BACK, PRESSED:

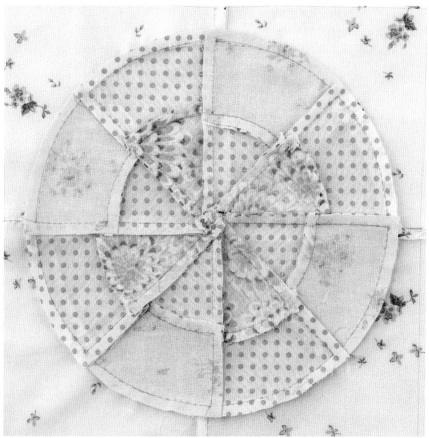

23

SAILOR'S JOY

This block is a quirky take on the classic eight-point star. For a variation and to create a kaleidoscopic effect, cut the centre from a stripy fabric and use a good dark fabric for the points to emphasize the design.

METHOD

1 Alternating the colours, stitch the A pieces to the B pieces. Make eight in total, four in one colour scheme and four in the other colour scheme.

2 Stitch two A+B units together in pairs, alternating the colours. Make four pairs in total.

3 Stitch two pairs together to make a 'half' section. Repeat to join the other two pairs.

4 Stitch the halves together.

5 Set in the C and D pieces, starting with the C pieces.

6 Press.

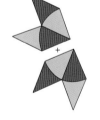

Making the sampler quilt

I made four Sailor's Joy blocks for my quilt (see page 94), two in one colourway and two in another. If you would like to do this, you will need to multiply the cutting amounts by 4, or by 2 in colourway 1 and by 2 in colourway 2.

Finished size

9in (23cm) square

Cut

From background/ light-coloured fabric:

▸ four D pieces

▸ four C pieces

From medium-/ dark-coloured fabric:

▸ eight B pieces, four in colour 1 and four in colour 2

▸ eight A pieces, four in colour 1 and four in colour 2

Templates

Shown smaller here and in colour for reference.
For actual-size templates, see page 139.

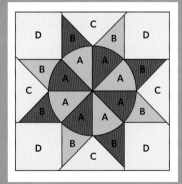

BLOCK FROM THE FRONT:

BLOCK FROM THE BACK, PRESSED:

24

CASSIOPIA

This block is a great scrap buster, so it's worth keeping every last scrap of fabric left over from other projects so they can be used in such a fun block. The gentle curves on the outer edge could create a wonderful secondary pattern if you choose to make a quilt entirely with repeats of this block. If you have a fabric from which to fussy cut the centre piece, this would be an added bonus to the overall design.

Finished size
12in (30.5cm) square

Cut
From background or light-coloured fabric:
▶ four C pieces
▶ four CR pieces

From medium-/ dark-coloured fabric:
▶ one A piece
▶ eight B pieces, from eight different fabrics
▶ eight BR pieces, from eight different fabrics

Templates
Shown smaller here and in colour for reference.
For actual-size templates, see page 140.

METHOD

1 Arrange the fabrics before stitching, so you can order your colours appropriately.

2 Stitch a B piece to a BR piece. Repeat to make eight pairs in total.

3 Stitch two pairs of B+BR units together. Make four 'quarter' sections in total.

4 Stitch the 'quarters' into two 'halves'.

5 Stitch the halves together.

6 Set in the A piece, at the centre.

7 Stitch a C piece to a CR piece to make a corner piece. Make four in total.

8 Set in the C+CR corner units around the centre.

9 Press.

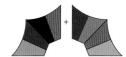

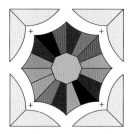

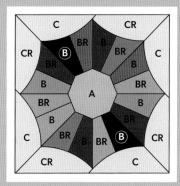

Making the sampler quilt

I made one Cassiopia block for my quilt (see page 94).

BLOCK FROM THE FRONT:

BLOCK FROM THE BACK, PRESSED:

25

TURKEY TRACKS

For the sampler quilt, I've made up four of this block and then split them up with sashing and a post (see page 97). There are lots of variations on this classic block. You could place the blocks all in a clockwise (or anti-clockwise direction) and then the Turkey would be walking in circles. If you choose the same fabrics as your block for the sashing and post, this will tie things together nicely.

METHOD

1 Stitch the F piece and the FR piece to either side of the C piece.

2 Set the D piece and the DR piece into the C+F+FR unit.

3 Stitch the E and ER pieces to either side of the B piece.

4 Stitch the A piece to B+E+ER unit.

5 Set one unit into the other.

6 Press.

7 I added sashing strips around the Turkey Tracks block for my final quilt, as well as a post square. See page 90 for more information about adding sashing strips and post squares.

Making the sampler quilt

I made four Turkey Tracks blocks for my quilt (see page 94). If you'd like to do this, you will need to multiply the cutting amounts by 4.

Finished size

8in (20.25cm) square

Cut

From background or light-coloured fabric:

- ▸ one E piece
- ▸ one ER piece
- ▸ one D piece
- ▸ one DR piece
- ▸ one A piece

From medium-/ dark-coloured fabric:

- ▸ one F piece in colour 1
- ▸ one FR piece in colour 1
- ▸ one C piece in colour 2
- ▸ one B piece in colour 1

Templates

Shown smaller here and in colour for reference.
For actual-size templates, see pages 138, 140 and 141.

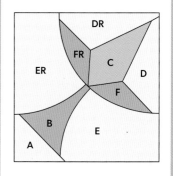

BLOCK FROM THE FRONT:

BLOCK FROM THE BACK, PRESSED:

26

THIRTIES TULIP

This is a lovely floral block based on one from a quilt in my collection from the 1930s. Floral and tulip blocks are often made with appliqué, so it's nice to have flower-inspired designs that can be pieced alongside the rest of the quilt. As with the Turkey Tracks block (see page 84), if you make up several you can play with the arrangement – in the case of the sampler quilt, I created a ring of flowers (see page 99).

METHOD

1 Stitch the B and BR pieces to either side of the C piece.

2 Stitch D and DR pieces to either side of the A piece.

3 Sew the B+BR+C and A+D+DR units together, setting into the other.

4 Stitch the E piece to the ER piece to make the top 'corner' unit.

5 Set the E+ER 'corner' section into the top of the unit.

6 Press.

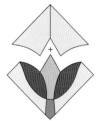

Making the sampler quilt

I made four Thirties Tulip blocks for my quilt (see page 94), in two different colourways. If you'd like to do this, you will need to multiply the cutting amounts by 4, or by 2 for colourway 1 and 2 for colourway 2.

Finished size
9in (23cm) square

Cut
From background or light-coloured fabric:
▶ one E piece
▶ one ER piece
▶ one D piece
▶ one DR piece

From medium-/ dark-coloured fabric:
▶ one B piece
▶ one BR piece
▶ one C piece
▶ one A piece

Templates
Shown smaller here for reference. For actual-size templates, see page 142.

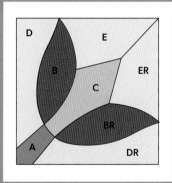

BLOCK FROM THE FRONT:

BLOCK FROM THE BACK, PRESSED:

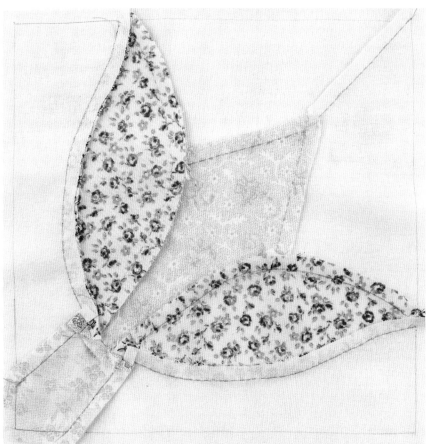

27

SUNBURST

This block is well worth the stitching time and is surprisingly straightforward given its showstopping effect. Cut the pieces and pin carefully to line up all those points, to ensure you have a neat and precise final block.

Finished size
15in (38cm) square

Cut
From background or light-coloured fabric:
▸ four E pieces
▸ sixteen C pieces

From medium-/ dark-coloured fabric:
▸ one A piece
▸ sixteen B pieces
▸ sixteen D pieces

Templates
Shown smaller here and in colour for reference.
For actual-size templates, see pages 143 and 144.

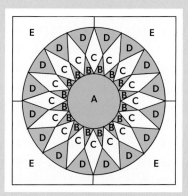

Making the sampler quilt
I made one Sunburst block for my quilt (see page 94).

1

METHOD

1 Stitch a B piece and a D piece to either side of a C piece. Repeat to make sixteen trios in total.

2 Stitch the units together into a circle.

3 Set the A piece into the centre to complete the circle unit.

4 Stitch the E pieces together in pairs to make two 'frame' sections.

5 Stitch the two 'frames' together.

6 Set the circle into the frame. Mark the midpoint along the curve of each 'E' shape, fold the fabric in half, and pinch the midpoint between your fingers, pinning at each quarter and finger pressing at the eighth points to fit and ease in the circle unit neatly.

7 Press.

2
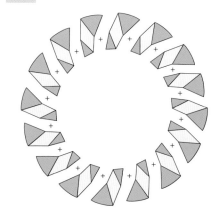

3
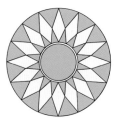

6
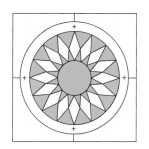

BLOCK FROM THE FRONT:

BLOCK FROM THE BACK, PRESSED:

ADDING **SASHING & POST SQUARES**

Sashing comprises strips of fabric placed between or around blocks to fit them together into a quilt or, in our quilt here, to increase their size. The sashing that has been added to the Turkey Tracks (page 84) and the Pansy (page 60) blocks makes the blocks the size needed to fit with the other units, as well as adding a design feature.

Post squares, or corner stones, are often used to break up long pieces of sashing. As well as adding a design element, they make it easier to fit the blocks and sashing together as the seams will form convenient junctions. In the Turkey Tracks block, I've taken the post colour from one of the colours used in the block to provide a focal point and enhance the design.

SASHING STRIPS

1 Cut out the sashing strips from fabric using the necessary templates.

2 Find the midpoint of one edge of the block and the sashing strip: do this by folding in half and finger pressing each piece. Now pin these together as you have done with your patches: pin at each end first, then together in the middle, and then the quarter points in between. If you need to ease any fabric to fit, then it can be done between these pinned points.

3 Stitch as usual, following your sewing line and removing pins as you go.

4 Press the seams towards the sashing.

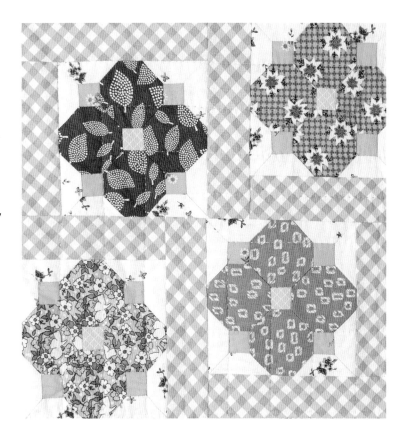

POST SQUARES, OR CORNER STONES

These squares will usually be sewn between long pieces of sashing before being used to join rows of blocks together.

1 Cut out the square from fabric using the template.

2 Pin a square to the short end of a sashing strip and sew in place.

3 Add a second sashing strip to the other side of the post square.

4 Press both seams towards the sashing.

5 Now use this strip between the two rows of blocks and sew them together. Press towards the sashing.

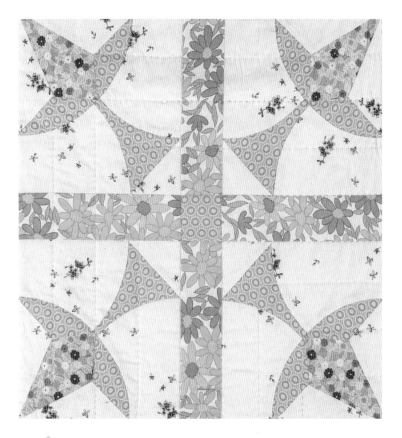

MAKING THE QUILT
YOUR OWN

The block combinations in my quilt all combine to make 'units' measuring 18in (45.75cm) square. You can combine any block you like to do this, using filler strips if you need to. It's fun to have a play around before committing to stitching the blocks together.

By all means, place the blocks in the positions shown in the arrangements on pages 94 and 95. But you may have noticed that some of the blocks are the same size, and the sizes of some of the smaller blocks can be combined to make up the sizes of the larger blocks. With this information, it is easy to substitute one block, or multiple blocks, for another, and give your quilt its own personality – see the table opposite.

Block size	Large block designs	Smaller block substitutes
6in (15.25cm) square blocks	Album (page 44) Bright Hopes (page 46) Spools (page 48) Bow Tie (page 50) Snowball (page 52) Mill & Star (page 54)	4 x Half Square Triangle (page 38) – 3in (7.5cm) square 4 x Kansas Dugout (page 40) – 3in (7.5cm) square 2 x Flying Geese (page 42) – 3 x 6in (7.5 x 15.25cm)
8in (20.25cm) square blocks	Turkey Tracks (page 84)	4 x Four Patch (page 36) – 4in (10cm) square
9in (23cm) square blocks	Sailor's Joy (page 80) Thirties Tulip (page 86)	9 x Half Square Triangle (page 38) – 3in (7.5cm) square 6 x Kansas Dugout (page 40) – 3in (7.5cm) square
10in (25.5cm) square blocks	Wishing Star (pages 66) Arrowhead (page 72)	25 x 2in (5cm) squares from the Two Patch & Four Patch block (page 36) – 2in (5cm) square
12in (30.5cm) square blocks	Woven Ribbons (page 58) Grandmother's Star (page 62) Western Star (page 64) Drusilla's Delight (page 68) Southern Star (page 70) Marbles (page 76) Water Wheel (page 78) Cassiopia (page 82)	4 x any of the 6in (15.25cm) square blocks (see above) 16 x Half Square Triangle (page 38) – 3in (7.5cm) square 16 x Kansas Dugout (page 40) – 3in (7.5cm) square 8 x Flying Geese (page 42) – 3 x 6in (7.5 x 15.25cm) 6 x Four Patch (page 36) – 4in (10cm) square
15in (38cm) square blocks	Sunburst (page 88)	15 x Half Square Triangle (page 38) – 3in (7.5cm) square 15 x Kansas Dugout (page 40) – 3in (7.5cm) square
18in (45.75cm) square blocks	Courthouse Steps (pages 56) Carpenter's Wheel (pages 74)	6 x any of the 6in (15.25cm) square blocks (see above) 4 x any of the 9in (22.75cm) square blocks (see above)

QUILT SAMPLER LAYOUTS

Sampler quilt – main design

Blocks

1 Two Patch (page 36)

2 Half Square Triangle (page 38)

3 Kansas Dugout (page 40)

4 Flying Geese (page 42)

5 Album (page 44)

6 Bright Hopes (page 46)

7 Spools (page 48)

8 Bow Tie (page 50)

9 Snowball (page 52)

10 Mill & Star (page 54)

11 Courthouse Steps (page 56)

12 Woven Ribbons (page 58)

13 Pansy (page 60)

14 Grandmother's Star (page 62)

15 Western Star (page 64)

Sampler quilt – variation

SEWING **THE QUILT** TOGETHER

You can stitch the blocks together now. Remember: if you have swapped any blocks around, or substituted some, make sure to include those changes here.

Depending on the size of block, the blocks have been stitched together in sections to form 18in (45.75cm) square 'units'. (Note: since the Carpenter's Wheel block measures this already, it is its own unit.) I have numbered these units from 1 to 16 (see the plan below), and we'll be working from the top-left unit.

Using the blocks indicated in each unit's instructions, follow the piecing order diagrams to create the units from the sampler quilt.

Unit 1

Blocks used:

▸ one Southern Star (page 70)

▸ five Bow Tie (page 50)

Piecing order:

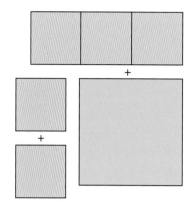

Unit 2

Blocks used:

▸ four Turkey Tracks (page 84)

▸ four sashing strips (see page 90), using the template on page 141

▸ one post square (see page 90), using the template on page 130

Piecing order:

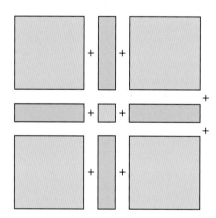

Unit 3

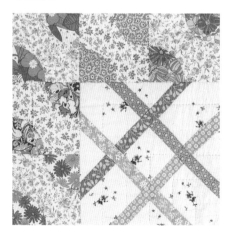

Blocks used:

▸ one Woven Ribbons (page 58)

▸ five Snowball (page 52)

Piecing order:

As per Unit 1.

Unit 4

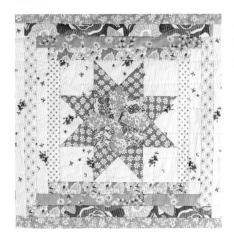

Blocks used:
▸ one Wishing Star (page 66)
▸ one Courthouse Steps (page 56)

Piecing order:
Not applicable (as is).

Unit 5

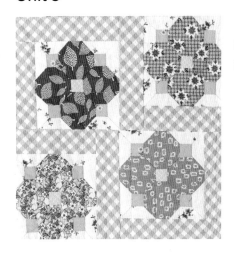

Blocks used:
▸ four Pansy (page 60)
▸ four sashing strips (see page 90), using the template on page 134

Piecing order:

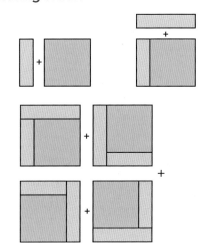

Unit 6

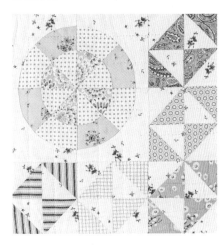

Blocks used:
▸ one Water Wheel (page 78)
▸ twenty Half Square Triangles (page 38), joined to make five Broken Dish units

Piecing order:

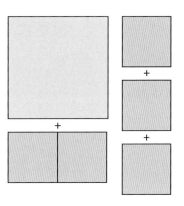

Unit 7

Blocks used:

▶ four Thirties Tulip (see page 86)

Piecing order:

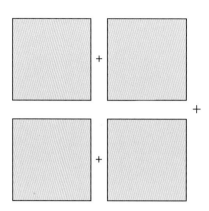

Unit 8

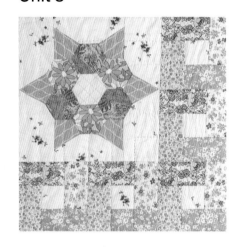

Blocks used:

▶ one Grandmother's Star (page 62)
▶ five Bright Hopes (page 46)

Piecing order:

As per Unit 6 (see opposite).

Unit 9

Blocks used:

▶ one Cassiopia (page 82)
▶ five Album (page 44)

Piecing order:

As per Unit 1 (see page 97).

Unit 10

Blocks used:

▸ one Carpenter's Wheel (page 74)

Piecing order:

Not applicable (as is).

Unit 11

Blocks used:

▸ one Drusilla's Delight (page 68)

▸ five Spools (page 48)

Piecing order:

As per Unit 1 (see page 97).

Unit 12

Blocks used:

▸ one Sunburst (page 88)

▸ eleven Kansas Dugout (page 40)

Piecing order:

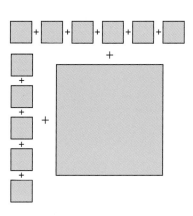

Unit 13

Blocks used:

▸ one Arrowhead (page 72)

▸ twenty-eight Two Patch (page 36)

Piecing order:

Side sections –

Top and bottom sections –

Unit 14

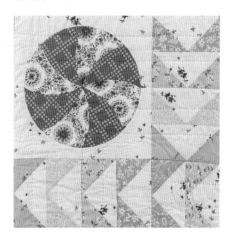

Blocks used:
▸ one Marbles (page 76)
▸ ten Flying Geese (page 42)

Piecing order:
As per Unit 6 (see page 98).

Unit 15

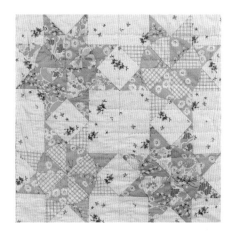

Blocks used:
▸ four Sailor's Joy (page 80)

Piecing order:
As per Unit 7 (see page 99).

Unit 16

Blocks used:
▸ one Western Star (page 64)
▸ five Mill & Star (page 54)

Piecing order:
As per Unit 6 (see page 98).

SEWING THE UNITS TOGETHER

The units go together in four rows of four. It is also worth mentioning here that if you want to sew the quilt using an appropriate Quilt As You Go method, this is when you could do that (see the tip box below).

If you are sewing the quilt top in the traditional fashion as I have done for the sampler in this book, then sew the rows of four units, and press the seams in alternating directions: this is so they will knit together neatly.

Once the rows are ready, stitch them together to make the quilt top. Press the seams in one direction.

Give your quilt top a final press. The next step is to layer it with wadding/batting and backing fabric, then quilt it (see pages 104–121)

What is Quilt As You Go?

This is simply quilting each block before sewing them together, rather than sewing all the blocks together before quilting.

For this method, you will need to make mini quilt sandwiches for each unit before quilting. This means cutting backing fabric and wadding/batting so they are larger than the unit (this is approx. 20in/50.75cm square for our sampler quilt), then tacking/basting them together with the unit in the centre (see pages 109–114 for more on this). You are, essentially, then treating your QAYG blocks like mini quilts. For many people this is a more manageable approach to quilting a quilt, and makes the whole project more portable too.

There are a number of different methods to choose when sewing the quilted blocks together, and these can be found in books like *Quilt As You Go* (Carolyn Forster , Search Press, 2021).

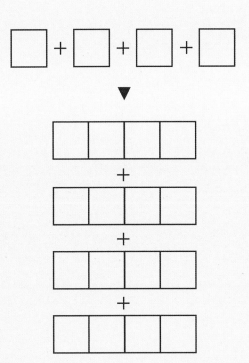

TACKING/BASTING & QUILTING **NECESSITIES**

Once you have sewn your patchwork top, the next stage is to create what is known as a quilt sandwich. This is when the quilt top and backing fabric are layered together, with the wadding/batting placed in between.

Thread

TACKING/BASTING THREAD

Use a specialist tacking/basting thread as this breaks easily and is cheaper than regular sewing thread, but holds the layers together securely enough for quilting.

QUILTING THREAD

▸ This will be thread that will form the quilting stitches, and in turn hold the three layers of the quilt together. Quilting thread is slightly thicker than general sewing thread.

▸ Choose a colour that blends with the overall appearance of the quilt (see the thread colours I often use in the photo below), unless you want the stitches to stand out on particular areas.

▸ Fine hand-quilting thread is usually sold on spools marked as such, and will usually be 28wt. The reels that you buy will say on them that they are for hand or machine quilting (sometimes they will work well for both). Different manufacturers may vary their recommendations slightly, but it is always worth trying a new thread to see which brand you prefer.

▸ If you choose to hand quilt with big-stitch quilting, which has bigger, bolder stitches, then you will need to use a thicker thread. Thicker thread also quilts up faster than regular hand-quilting thread. Popular threads for big-stitch quilting are Coton Perle no. 8 or no. 12, Coton à Broder size 16 and Aurifil 12wt.

Needles

TACKING/BASTING NEEDLES

A longer needle is often useful for this process. Again, some makes will brand the needles as 'basting needles', making it easy to see their purpose. I generally use Cotton Darners (also known as Long Darners) size 7 for tacking/basting.

QUILTING NEEDLES

▸ These are usually short needles with a round eye. The packet will be labelled as 'Betweens' or 'quilting needles', so that they are easy to identify.

▸ Needles come in a range of sizes to accommodate different thread weights/types and skill levels. Use the size that is comfortable in your hand. Sometimes the needle size you need will be down to practice, and sometimes it'll depend on the combination of fabrics and wadding/batting!

▸ For fine hand quilting you'll want to use smaller needles – the smaller the needle you use, the smaller your stitches will be. If you're a beginner, start with a size 8 Betweens needle then aim to work up to using a size 10 or 11.

▸ For big-stitch quilting, which uses a thicker thread, you can use a Betweens size 6, an embroidery needle size 6, a Sashiko needle (often sold in mixed-size packets) or a Chenille needle size 22.

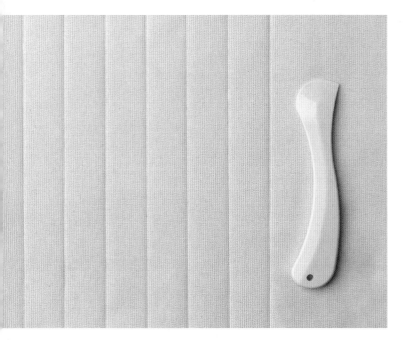

Hera marker

My favourite way to mark my quilts is with a Hera marker. This is a small plastic tool of Japanese origins. Similar things can be found in British and North American quilt making. Bodkins embedded in a cork for ease of holding, and even your fingernail, can be used to score the fabric, leaving a crease that you can follow with your quilting stitch. Any creasing method is non-invasive and uses no inks, so there is no worry about harmful chemicals or needing to get rid of the marks afterwards. When the quilt is washed, any creases that weren't quilted over will disappear.

Masking tape

Using basic low-tack masking tape from a DIY shop is another easy way to mark quilting lines. Use your ruler as a guide, and instead of scoring with a Hera marker, gently stick the tape to the quilt. The quilting can be worked along the side of the tape. The tape is easily removed, and in some cases can be re-used a few times before its tackiness is lost. Be careful not to leave tape on a quilt when not working on it, especially close to a heater or radiator, as heat and time can affect the glue and the tape may mark the fabric.

Safety pins with covers

For safety-pin tacking/basting (see page 112). Some people find it easier to on the hands to use pins with covers, as these make them simpler to open and grip.

Quilting hoop

For large quilts (i.e., anything bigger than a pillow cover), I use a quilting hoop. These are generally wooden and 1in (2.5cm) deep, and the most common and useful size is one that is 14in (35.5cm) in diameter. Don't try to quilt with an embroidery hoop, as these are too shallow and your work will pop out. A hoop will act like a third hand for you. It will be something that holds the quilt for you, allowing your two hands to work on the stitches.

Teaspoon or grapefruit spoon

To help ease the needle up through the layers when tacking/basting, use a teaspoon or a grapefruit spoon. See more on pages 110 and 114.

Thimbles/finger protection

You should be used to protecting your fingers by now from the hand piecing, and you will find it an advantage to continue with this while you quilt. Pushing the needle through all the layers requires extra force, and using some form of protection will make the quilting process easier. Take a look back to page 23 for ideas and more information.

BACKING FABRIC

- ▶ Choose a fabric that is a similar weight to those used on the front of the quilt. As you are hand quilting, you will want a fabric that will be easy to work with (see page 9 for information on quilt-top fabrics).

- ▶ The backing fabric can be patterned or plain. If you choose plain, remember that your quilting stitches will be highly visible; a patterned fabric will hide them. If you decide to use your backing fabric for self-bound binding (see page 127), this will impact what fabric you use too.

- ▶ The backing fabric will need to be wider and longer than the patchwork top. This is in order to accommodate shrinkage or the 'pulling up' of the quilt top and wadding/batting when you quilt. The surplus backing fabric (and wadding/batting) will be trimmed off when you bind the quilt.

- ▶ If you choose fabric that will need joining, follow these basic points: remove the selvedges/selvages from the sides of the fabric (see page 18). Sew the seam using a ¼in or ⅜in (5mm or 1cm) SA, and press the seam open. This will reduce the bulky areas you need to quilt through.

- ▶ From the diagrams, right, you can see that the backing fabric can be pieced and seamed vertically (**A**), horizontally (**B**) or you can cut one of the lengths of backing of fabric in half lengthways and join it to either side of the wider piece (**C**). Some people prefer this method so that when you fold the quilt the seams do not come under so much stress.

- ▶ You can buy special wide-width fabrics for backing fabric. This means you won't need to join your fabrics, saving you from having seams on the back of the quilt.

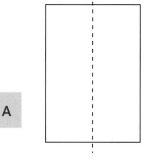

A

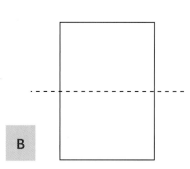

B

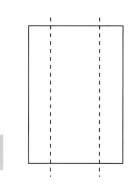

C

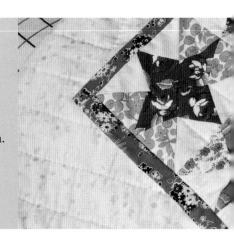

Quantity needed for sampler quilt

- ▶ **Overall fabric needed:** 164in (4.25m) x WOF

- ▶ **Cutting requirements:** cut this into two equal lengths. Remove the selvedge/selvage (see page 18) and stitch together along the length with a ⅜in (1cm) SA. Press open.

WADDING/BATTING

Wadding/batting is the puffy bit that goes between the patchwork top and the backing fabric. It can be made from polyester, cotton, or a combination of these two; wool; sustainably grown bamboo; recycled plastic bottles; or even an old clean blanket or a flannelette sheet.

The important things to think about when choosing your wadding are how 'puffy' you want the quilt to be and how much quilting you want to do.

This puffiness is called 'loft' and gives the quilt its characteristic look. Low-loft waddings are great for traditional, thin quilts. Medium-loft waddings are puffier and can be machine or hand quilted. High-loft waddings are more difficult to machine quilt.

All waddings will say on the wrapper how far apart you can leave the quilting lines. If you did not want to do much quilting, then a wadding that recommends 10in (25.5cm) between each quilt line would be a good choice. For more quilting, then you could choose a wadding that needs quilting every 2–4in (5–10cm).

I encourage you to ask other quilters what they use, too. If they have an odd off-cut, they are usually pleased to share it with you; this means you can have a try out before buying.

Joining wadding/batting pieces

If your piece of wadding/batting isn't large enough, you can join several pieces together. You can do this by using a product like HeatnBond®, with large zigzag stitches sewn on the sewing machine, or sewn by hand with baseball/suture stitch. Suture stitch pulls both sides of the wadding together evenly, and allows them to lay flat. If stitching, use a neutral thread colour that will not show through the front of your quilt. Always make sure that the two edges do no not overlap; they just need to butt together.

BASEBALL/SUTURE STITCH

1 Start with a knot on the WS and a backstitch to secure the thread in the wadding/batting. Bring the needle up on one side of the wadding/batting, ¼in (5mm) or so away from the central gap.

2 Bring the needle up on the other side of the gap, a little further along than your previous stitch so they're slightly offset.

3 Repeat this motion of coming up from the centre and alternating left and right. In this way, the stitch evenly pulls the edges of the wadding/batting together.

4 Finish off with a few backstitches in the wadding/batting to secure.

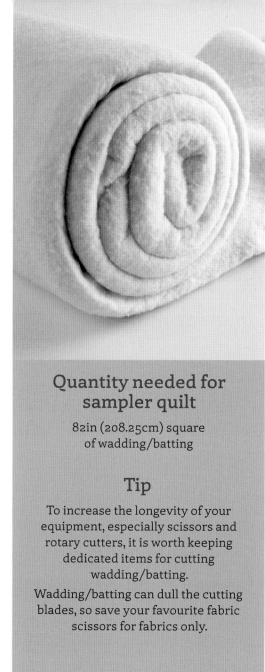

Quantity needed for sampler quilt

82in (208.25cm) square of wadding/batting

Tip

To increase the longevity of your equipment, especially scissors and rotary cutters, it is worth keeping dedicated items for cutting wadding/batting.

Wadding/batting can dull the cutting blades, so save your favourite fabric scissors for fabrics only.

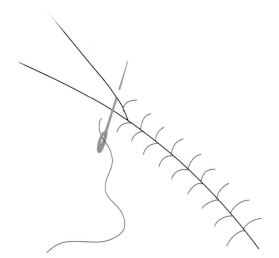

TACKING/BASTING
THE QUILT

In preparation for layering and tacking/basting the quilt, press the quilt top and backing fabric. If you can, leave them somewhere flat so that they will not need a second pressing (draped over a spare bed or stair rail is ideal). Unfold the wadding/batting the day before, to allow it to relax so that any creases can fall out. If you leave the wadding/batting in a steamy bathroom overnight this works well, or, if you run out of time, put the wadding/batting in the tumble dryer on the refresh cycle and this will do the same job!

HOLDING THE LAYERS TOGETHER FOR QUILTING

By trying the different methods on the following pages, you will find one that suits you and your quilt; often this will depend on the quilt in question.

Think about the way that the quilt will be quilted before you tack/baste it. Depending on the way that you quilt, you may not even need to tack/baste the layers together. For example, if you use a stand-up traditional frame with rollers, this will eliminate the tacking/basting process completely. Consider this option if you have the space at home and enjoy hand quilting in one particular place, as these are not easy to shift from one room to another!

If you use a circular hoop then safety-pin tacking/basting (see page 112) might not be the best choice. This is because the pins tend to get in the way of the hoop and need moving every time you reposition the hoop. If you are happy to keep doing this, then go ahead! It bothers some people but not others, so it is worth being aware before you start.

When you lap quilt, you do not have the additional stability that a hoop gives the work, so a little denser tacking/basting will stop the layers from shifting. For lap quilting, think about tacking/basting perhaps every 4in (10cm) rather than 6in (15cm). Use your closed fist as a gauge between tacking/basting lines, rather than a spread hand.

I often tack/baste the quilts on a carpeted floor, which helps the layers not to shift. If you have smooth floors, be aware that they may need protection as the needle going through can damage the floor. Either protect the floor by using a rotary-cutting mat between the backing and the floor, and moving it as you tack/baste, or perhaps table basting would work out better for you and your floor.

Tips

▸ Use a flat floor that is already clear where the quilt will lay out flat. If you don't have the space, you can use community and church halls – just make sure to book the space when you know the cleaner has just been! This saves you having to move your own furniture around to make room for the quilt on the floor.

▸ For any tacking/basting done on the floor, consider using a kneeling mat or knee pads to protect your knees during the process.

▸ Using a carpeted floor will stop the quilt moving too much. The edges can also be secured with masking tape.

▸ Use large tables if kneeling on the floor is not an option. Community and church halls often have these, if you don't have one at home.

▸ Use the services of a long-arm quilter: many offer a tacking/basting service, which lets you sit down and enjoy the quilting. This thread tacked/basted method offers all the advantages of manageability and no added weight, but with someone else having done the work.

Hand tacking/basting a quilt gives you the best control over the layers of the quilt and does not add any extra weight or bulk. Use specialist tacking/basting thread for ease (see page 105). Tack/baste the quilt in rows that are 6in (15cm) apart.

Regular hand tacking/basting

▸ Start with a knot and a backstitch, then work backstitch from right to left on the quilt (left to right if you are left-handed).

▸ The stitches should be about ½in (1.25cm) long and evenly spaced (see the diagram below; the dashed lines indicate the thread and stitches below the fabric).

▸ Finish with a backstitch to keep the thread secure.

▸ As the needle and your hands are always on the top of the quilt, your fingers can get sore as the needle pushes up against them. Using a teaspoon or a grapefruit spoon helps ease the needle up through the layers, and makes the process quicker. As you take the needle through the layers, simply push the needle up against the edge of a teaspoon or grapefruit spoon (see image below left).

Tailor tacking/basting

▸ Some people find the action of tacking/basting uncomfortable, as the needle is held horizontally to your body. If this is the case for you, try tacking/basting diagonally, known as tailor tacking/basting: the needle is held so it points towards your body, which can feel a more natural position.

▸ To tailor tack, thread the needle with tacking/basting thread and knot the end. Work the stitch from right to left (left to right if you are left-handed). Create rows of ½–1in (1.25–2.5cm) long diagonal stitches, depending on the length of the needle. Finish with a backstitch.

Using a teaspoon.

Regular hand tacking/basting.

Tailor's tacking.

TACKING/BASTING SYSTEMS

Generally, for all methods of tacking/basting, the securing method should form a grid, often dictated by the patches in the quilt. There should not usually be a gap bigger than 6in (15cm) between the tacking/basting stitches – about the size of your spread hand. If the patchwork does not have a grid to follow, use your hand span as a ready guide. I find it easier to work to a grid system when tacking/basting. As I always use the same system, I don't have to think or plan – just tack/baste!

Below is the way I hand tack/baste my quilts when they are on the floor. It smooths out wrinkles and flattens any puffs that may arise. Tools to make it quicker or more comfortable include thimbles, spoons, masking tape and a kneeling mat or knee pads.

1 Press the backing fabric and lay it on the floor WS upwards. Pat it flat. Secure to the floor with tabs of masking tape at the corners and the mid-points on all four sides. Do NOT stretch the fabric. If you stretch the fabric, it will retract back to its natural position when the masking tape comes off and the backing that is, by then, tacked/basted together in the quilt will start to pucker. We do not want that!

2 Lay the wadding/batting on top of the backing fabric. If it helps, fold the wadding/batting into four and line up the outside edge with the corner of the backing fabric then unfold a quarter at a time. This way, the middle of the backing and wadding/batting are central and you don't spend time re-adjusting the layers. Pat it flat.

3 Press the patchwork top for the last time. Now place the patchwork on top of the wadding/batting, RS up. Again fold into quarters if this helps. As your backing and wadding/batting will usually be slightly larger than your quilt top, you will be left with a margin all the way around. Pat flat. Add some tabs of masking tape at the corners.

4 Pin the three layers together in the centre, at the corners and the mid-point on each side. This is just to keep things in place while you tack/baste.

5 If you are hand tacking/basting, start with a knot and a backstitch to secure your thread. Start by tacking/basting the diagonals (**A**). If necessary, use a teaspoon to bring the needle up out of the quilt for ease, or use your thimble to protect your fingers. Finish with a backstitch. You never need to have your hand under the quilt; you are working from the top all of the time. This way you do not disturb the layers.

6 Tack/baste across the middle in both directions (**B**). Remove the pins as you come across them.

7 Using your hand span as a guide, tack/baste in rows from the centre, working towards the outside edge (**C**). When this section is full, move round to the next (**D**). There are four sections to fill in this way, always starting from the middle and working towards the outside edge (**E** and **F**).

8 When complete, tack/baste ¼in (5mm) away from the outside edge of the quilt sandwich. This will eventually be removed, as the quilt gradually shifts when you quilt it, but in the meantime will stop the edges getting tatty or stretched.

9 Remove the masking tape, and pick up the quilt (and yourself) from the floor! If you like, you can now fold over the extra wadding/batting and backing fabric and tack/baste it abutting the edge of the quilt.

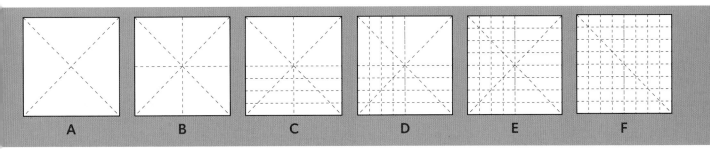

A   B   C   D   E   F

SAFETY-PIN TACKING/BASTING

Using safety pins is a fast way to get your quilt layers tacked/basted. Some people find the pins with pin covers easier on the hands – they give you something bigger to get hold of, and 'magically' the open pins do not stick together in clumps when stored.

1 Lay out the quilt sandwich, but do not pin. Starting from the centre of the quilt, and from the top/RS, use the safety pins to hold the layers together. Insert the pin and bring it back up through all three layers. This is where a grapefruit spoon will ease the fingers as you bring the point of the pin up against their edge and clip the pin closed.

2 The pins should be placed neither too closely nor too far from each other. Use your clenched fist as a gauge for pin placement – about 6in (15cm) apart.

3 When the quilt is covered with pins, tack around the edge as described in step 8 on page 111.

Safety pins with covers.

TABLE-TOP TACKING/BASTING

Learning to tack/baste on a table top will save you crawling around on the floor, and often having to clear the space in the first place. It will mean that you can sit and work in relative comfort without the worry of sore knees or putting a room out of use while you use the floor space. The table does not have to be as big as the quilt – you can use a large dining table, a table-tennis table or a wallpaper pasting table. I use a 24 x 31in (61 x 79cm) collapsible picnic table that folds away for easy storage.

You will need

▸ **One table at a comfortable height:**
I'm using a picnic table with a smooth surface. If you are using a dining table, make sure it's protected with a thick cloth or cutting mat, so the table doesn't get marked by the pins or clamps. If the table is not high enough to work at comfortably, invest in some plastic piping that will fit on to the bottom of the legs, increasing the height. Piping can be cut easily with a hacksaw. Table risers are also good for adjusting the table height

▸ **Chair:** I use an office chair, so I can adjust the height as I tack/baste

▸ **Masking tape**

▸ **Cocktail sticks (tooth picks)**

▸ **Bulldog clips or spring clamps**

1 Measure and mark the centre of the table with a cross, and mark the halfway points on each side of the table. Then, re-mark these positions by sticking a cocktail stick/toothpick on top using masking tape. For the centre mark, stick one in place, then cut another in half, and stick down to the table. These will need to be removed before you actually tack/baste, but you need them initially to feel the centre of the table when the fabric and wadding/batting is positioned. Some people just put the sticks on the outside edge of the table, as they are easier to remove. After some practice you will see what works best for you.

2 Press the backing fabric and fold it into quarters, wrong sides together. Place it on the table in one quarter section – the right side of the fabric will be facing you and, as you unfold it, the wrong side will be uppermost.

3 Unfold the backing fabric. Line up the edges with the points on the sides of the table so as to keep it straight.

4 Use bulldog clips or clamps to secure the fabric to the edges of the table. If the quilt is smaller than the table, the edges that don't overhang can be taped into place. There is no need to stretch the fabric – it just needs to lay flat, and this is done by gently patting the fabric and securing in place with a clamp at each corner. If the fabric is stretched, when the clamps are undone, the fabric will release and make ripples.

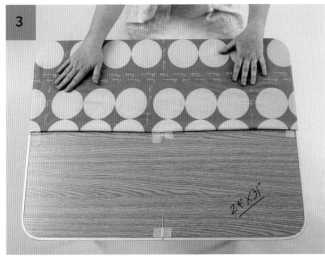

5 Now fold the wadding/batting in the same way and place on top of the backing fabric. You can feel the cocktail stick markers through the backing fabric, so you can use these to ensure the wadding/batting is squared up and central on the backing. Smooth the wadding/batting by patting gently, without stretching it. Replace the clips already in position to hold both layers in place.

Continued overleaf > > >

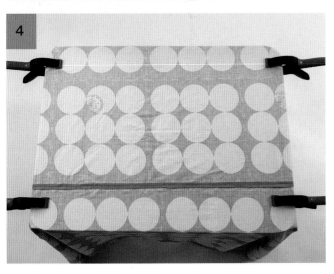

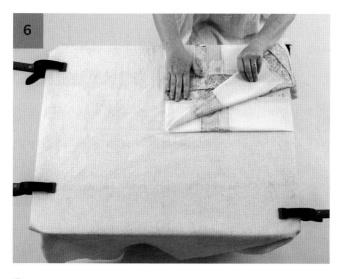

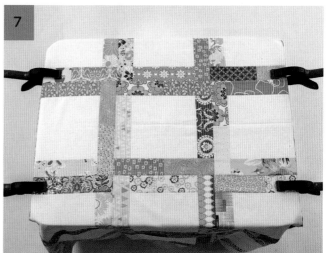

6 Press the quilt top and fold it into quarters, wrong side facing out. Match the centre of the top to the centre of the wadding/batting, and unfold as for the other layers. The quilt top will now be right side up.

7 Pat the fabric smooth and use the clips or clamps to hold the three layers together. You can now carefully remove the cocktail sticks if you like, or wait until you need to move the quilt to tack/baste the next section.

8 Tack/baste the area that is being held on the table, as per step 2 of 'Safety pin tacking/basting' on page 112. One of the keys to tacking/basting with thread or safety pins is only working from the front of the quilt. If you find it hard to push the needle or the pin heads up from the table, use a teaspoon.

9 When the area of the quilt on top of the table is complete, take off the clips (and tape if using) and shift the layers towards or away from you so the next untacked/unbasted area is on the table top.

10 Secure the side of the quilt that has been tacked/basted, then pat the backing flat and secure with clips. Make sure the wadding/batting is flat again on the backing and reposition the quilt top in place. Use tape if needed and replace the last two clamps. Tack/baste as before. Continue like this until the entire quilt is tacked/basted. You will need to move the quilt between three to nine times to completely tack/baste it. When this is complete, tack/baste ¼in (5mm) away from the outside edge all round the quilt top, as per step 8 on page 111.

HAND QUILTING

There are two kinds of hand quilting I like to use: fine hand quilting and big-stitch quilting. The method for both is the same; the only difference is the thickness of the thread and the size of the needles used.

Before we start stitching, make sure you know how to securely start and stop stitching (see page 118). This will stop you wasting time going back over stitches that have come undone.

The length of thread you work with should be no longer than your arm. This may not seem very long, but it will make it easier to stitch with. The thread is less likely to become tangled and knot, and creates a more ergonomic arm movement when stitching: instead of having to pull a long thread skywards, you will be pivoting from the elbow, which is a lot less tiring.

As you quilt, you can remove the tacking/basting stitches or pins as you work.

SETTING UP

Many of us will be hand quilting using a hoop. When you lay your quilt over the inner hoop and place the outer hoop on top, you will need to tighten the screw enough to hold the quilt firmly. As you tighten the screw, make sure that the quilt is flat with no pleats around the edge. You will also need to check that the quilt is not tight like a drum. There must be some movement in the quilt, so if you poke your finger up from underneath you will be able to make a hill and see the indentation of your fingernail. All of this will help you to be able to make the stitches.

When I work, the hand under the quilt, wearing a ridged thimble, pushes the quilt layers up to make a 'hill', which the needle will push against to make the stitch (see the bottom photograph in the tip box on page 117).

FINE HAND QUILTING

Sometimes known as 'little quilting', fine hand quilting is the traditional form of hand quilting with the emphasis being on making small, even running stitches to hold the three layers of the quilt together, and with it create a textured design all over the quilt. It's very similar to big-stitch quilting (opposite), except a smaller needle and finer thread is used.

Historically, it was considered important to make your stitches as small as possible, perhaps up to as many as 14 stitches to 1in (2.5cm). Nowadays, this 'rule' is less adhered to.

To start with you may want a larger size needle to work with, like the size 8. As you become more practiced, you can move on to one of the smaller sizes, such as the size 11. If these smaller needles prove harder to thread, then look out for 'easy thread' needles which will have a long eye.

NEEDLES:

▸ Betweens (quilting) sizes 8, 9, 10 and 11

THREAD:

▸ 28wt hand-quilting thread

For both quilt samplers (see pages 94 and 95) I used big-stitch quilting. Variegated warm grey-cream thread was used, which meant subtle shades of colour were introduced without fighting with the colours seen in the rest of the quilt.

BIG-STITCH QUILTING

This is a style of quilting that involves stitching with thicker thread and a larger needle, which means the stitches are bigger when compared to traditional fine hand quilting. The stitch length is often longer on the quilt top and smaller on the backing. The longer stitches and thicker thread of big-stitch quilting gives quilts a chunkier, naïve feel. It is sometimes referred to as Depression Stitch or 'Naïve Quilting'. Big-stitch quilting is a bolder, more relaxed style of quilting. The designs are usually widely spaced, therefore fewer lines of stitching are needed and – in turn – it takes less time to quilt. For these reasons, it tends to be a popular quilting choice.

NEEDLES:

▶ Embroidery size 6

▶ Betweens (quilting) size 6

▶ Sashiko, Chenille

THREAD:

▶ Coton Perle no. 8 or no. 12

▶ Coton à Broder size 16

▶ Aurifil 12wt

Quilting tips

▶ Follow the sequence on starting the stitch (see page 118) and continue on. As you make the stitches, try to work with a rhythm to create even but large stitches that go through all three layers of the quilt sandwich.

▶ Some people keep the needle hand still and move the finger that is on the underside of the quilt to create the stitches, while others do the opposite. Try different stitching motions to see which ones are comfortable for you, and create the evenly sized stitches you want.

▶ I find it helpful to have two thimbles: one on the middle finger of the needle hand for pushing the needle through, and another, ridged thimble on the index finger of the hand under the quilt.

▶ The finger under the quilt pushes the layers up, creating a little 'hill' with the ridge of the thimble (see image below, top) that the needle is pushed against to make the stitch (see image below, bottom).

▶ When you have about 6in (15cm) of thread left in the needle, I recommend finishing off and starting a new length of thread.

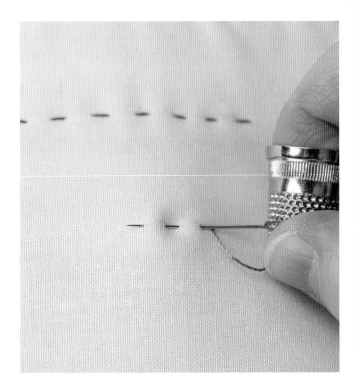

STARTING THE STITCH

Start by cutting a length of thread as long as your arm. Tie a knot in the end you just cut. Thread the free end into the needle. You need to insert the needle down through the top layer of fabric and wadding/batting then come up where you want to start, pulling on the thread so that the knot is embedded in the wadding/batting. The embedded thread will be quilted over, securing the thread further.

What if the knot won't pull through the fabric?

If the knot is stubborn, use the point of your sewing needle to poke open the weave of the fabric to expand the hole where the knot needs to go through. Gently pull the thread until the knot goes into the wadding/batting and then, using the needle again, push the threads back into place.

FINISHING THE STITCH

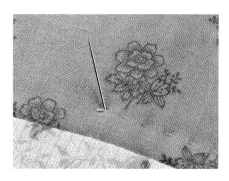

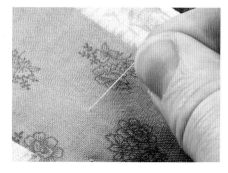

1 If the thread is running out, or you've finished your stitching, you will need to finish off securely. Make sure you leave enough thread – this will be about 5–6in (13–15cm) of thread. Make the last stitch, going all the way through to the back of the quilt with the needle, then bring the needle up at the beginning of the stitch.

2 Pull the thread through and wrap it around the needle two to three times, keeping the thread close to the quilt. (How many times you wrap the thread will depend on how thick it is and how densely woven the fabric is; you are making a knot that will pull through easily.)

3 Push the wrapped needle back through the fabric and into the wadding/batting, just underneath the middle of the last stitch, and travelling a needle's length away from the stitching. As you pull the thread a knot will form that needs to be gently pulled through to embed it in the wadding/batting. Snip the tail of thread close to the quilt top.

QUILTING DESIGNS

The designs I feel work best in a sampler-style quilt, like the quilt we are making, are ones that can be repeated and used all over the whole quilt. These repeatable designs are also easy to quilt if you do not have much quilting experience. If you are a more confident quilter, I would still opt for a design that will bring all the units in the quilt together.

Elbow quilting

I have used a design known as Elbow Quilting for the quilt sampler, as it fits nicely into each unit, covers the quilt evenly, is quick and simple to mark, and easy to stitch. It's found on lots of vintage quilts, and as an all-over quilting design it works well as it takes no notice of the patchwork itself. For the sampler, it fits neatly in the 18in (45.75cm) square units that make up the quilt (see pages 94–102), with the lines 2in (5cm) apart.

Here's how to mark the quilting lines:

1 Start with the block in the lower right-hand corner (or left-hand corner if you are left-handed). Position the square ruler in the bottom corner of the block, 2¼in (5.5cm) from the raw edge of the patchwork. This includes the ¼in (5mm) SA of the outside edge of the patchwork.

2 Mark the two sides of the square.

3 Move the ruler in towards the centre of the block, using the 2in (5cm) lines to match up with the first lines drawn. Mark the lines.

4 You may find that the 2in (5cm) lines you are marking coincide with seams in your patchwork. That is fine; you will still be quilting along these, even if you do not need to mark them.

5 Continue in this way until the 18in (45.75cm) square unit is covered. The last lines of quilting will be in the ditch around the seam of the entire unit.

6 Once one unit is marked, you can either move on to the next unit or quilt the one you've just marked. I like to mark then quilt each unit along the row until the bottom row is complete, then move to the next row up and repeat.

7 Continue in this way until the patchwork top is marked then quilted all over.

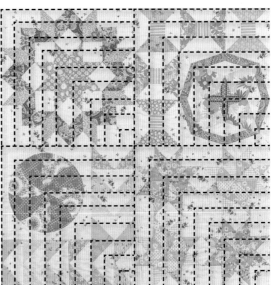

A section of the sampler quilt, indicating where the elbow stitching will fall.

Other quilting designs

AMISH WAVE

This is a curved design that is quilted all over the quilt, starting at an outside edge. It can be quilted in rows (**A**), or worked from the outside in (**B**). This is a popular choice of quilt design, and is ergonomic to quilt too. There are different ways for creating the wave design; the quickest and easiest is the method below, using your chosen circular household object.

1 Draw around a round object such as a plate, saucepan lid or pan onto a piece of paper.

2 Cut out the circle and fold into quarters.

3 Aligning the straight edges of the quarter-circle in the bottom right-hand corner of another sheet of card or template plastic, draw around the curve to create the first arc.

4 Unfold the paper to make a half circle and align with the bottom and right-hand edges of the paper. Draw around this shape, from the bottom left upwards, until the line of the second arc meets the line of the first arc.

5 Remove the paper circle.

6 Cut out the second shape, which is the template for the rest of the curves in your Amish Wave quilting.

7 Quilt lines within each wave, a needle-length apart and with each line gradually getting smaller (**C**).

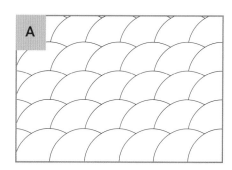

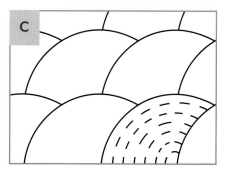

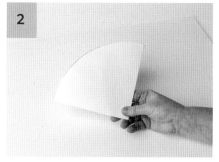

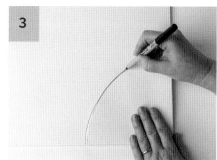

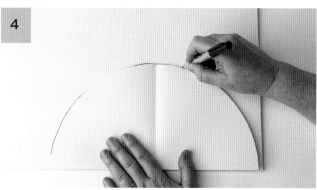

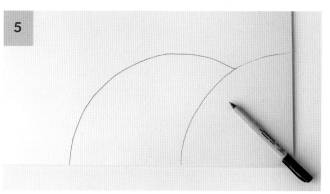

FAN ELBOW QUILTING

For this, hold the chalk in your right (or left) hand and place your elbow in the bottom right (or left) corner of the quilt. Using your elbow as the pivot point, draw a curve from one edge to the other. The second curve will be from where the first curve touches the bottom edge of the quilt and the centre top of the first curve. You will then fill these curves with quilted 'arches'.

   You can see why these large curves get their name. Each quilter will have a slightly different size curve, which will make each quilt's design truly individual.

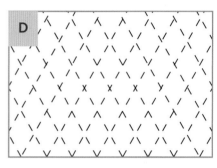

THUMB/EGG-CUP QUILTING

With this version use the round of your thumb to start in the corner of your quilt as above. You start by marking the smallest arch, using your thumb or an egg cup as a template, then add arches that increase in size as you work outwards. I usually work until I am happy with the size and number of arches. Then I count how many I stitched within a block, then stitch the same number in the blocks used in the rest of the quilt. Refer also to the Elbow Quilting method on page 119.

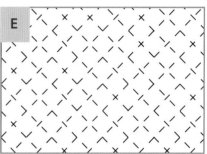

DIAGONAL LINES/CROSS-HATCHING

Lines and grids are easy to mark with a large rotary-cutting ruler and a Hera marker, or you could use masking tape. Decide which angle to use on the ruler and balance this up with the outside edge of the quilt. I tend to use 60-degree angles for my quilts (**D**), but 45-degree angles are popular (**E**). If you want to then mark a second set of lines from the other side of the quilt, then you will be able to form a grid or cross-hatched design (**F**).

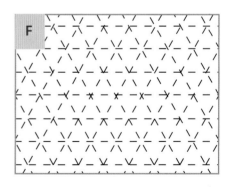

BINDING THE QUILT

Once your quilt is quilted, remove any remaining tacking/basting stitches and pins. It is now ready to bind.

This is the one point where you may want to consider a sewing machine, but it is by no means a necessity. You can follow all of the same steps below by sewing by hand. There will not be a great deal of difference in the finished quilt if you follow a few simple guidelines.

What I would suggest is that you use only backstitch for sewing on your binding, as the layers might be too bulky to sew with running stitch.

You can sew the seams with the same size needle and thread that you have pieced with: size 10 Sharps and 28wt thread. When you come to slip stitching the folded binding in place, you might want a thinner thread: I usually use a 40wt thread.

To prepare fabric for the wide square-corner binding for this quilt, you will need 36in (91.5cm) x width of fabric (WOF).

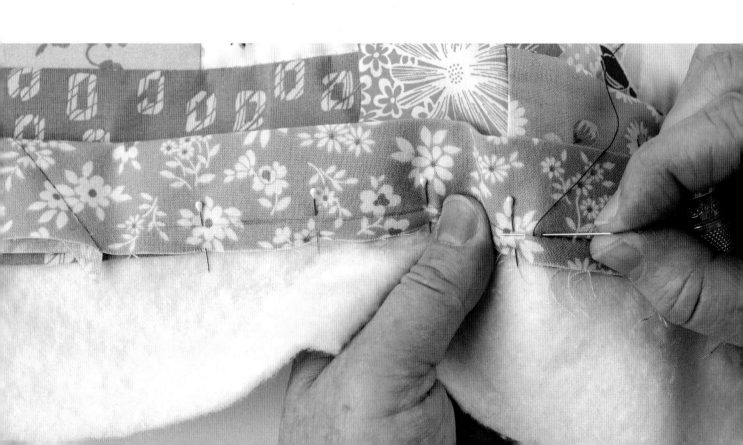

The binding for my quilts is most often made from strips of fabric cut across the width of the fabric. The strips of fabric will be folded over to make what is known as a 'double binding', which is very durable and gives a nice clean edge to your quilt.

Cutting strips from the width of fabric is an economical way to cut the binding and gives it a strong straight edge. The strips of fabric will need to be joined to make a continuous length. I use a bias or crossway join here to eliminate bulky areas when the binding is sewn and folded over the edge of the quilt.

Use the following method, whether you're cutting regular 2½in (6.5cm) strips for a regular width binding (see page 126) or 4½in (11.5cm) strips for the wide binding I have used on this sampler quilt (see pages 124 and 125).

Joining strips for binding

I use a bias join for joining strips together, which results in less bulk when the fabric is folded over and wrapped round the edge of the quilt.

1 Take one of the strips and lay another over the top, right sides together and at a 90-degree angle. Allow an extra ⅜in (1cm) of fabric along each short edge, as shown. Pin across the diagonal – you can mark in a stitch line with pencil or Hera marker, if you'd like a guide line.

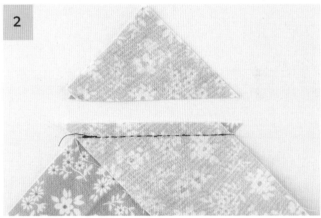

2 On the far-right end (or far-left end, if you are left-handed), make a backstitch, leaving the waste knot and tail visible on the WS facing you. Stitch small running stitches across the diagonal, making a backstitch about halfway along to anchor your running stitches. At the end, make a final backstitch then knot off. Cut off the excess fabric, leaving a ¼in (5mm) seam allowance. Repeat steps 1–3 to join together the remaining strips.

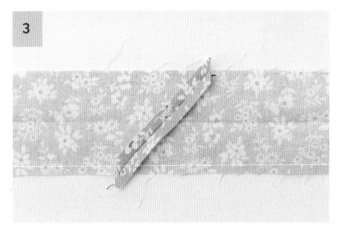

3 To finish your tape, open out the tape then press the seams open. I tend not to trim off the 'ears' of the seam allowances where the strips have been joined, as these will be hidden in the binding later. You can now press your tape in half, long edges and WS together.

HOW TO HAND SEW BINDING

The basic method for hand sewing binding to your quilt is by using backstitch. Sewing only with backstitch, rather than a combination of small running stitch and backstitch, will allow you to make bigger scoops of fabric, but still sew a small regular stitch, and accommodate the larger number of layers too.

1 You'll need to pin the binding to the quilt top, raw edges matching and with the binding facing towards the centre of the quilt top. Pin at 1in (2.5cm) intervals and, if you find it helpful, mark a ¼in (5mm) allowance from the raw edge of the binding to use a a stitch line guide. I do not usually trim the wadding/batting and backing to match the quilt until the tape has been applied to the quilt top. However, you could trim them at this stage if you wish.

2 Simply make a backstitch at the start of the of the binding, then work backstitch all along the marked stitch line.

3 Once the binding on the quilt-top side has been stitched in place, fold the binding over to the backing side. The binding on this side is stitched in place with slip stitch.

Hand-sewing the binding.

WIDE SQUARE-CORNER BINDING

This is a simple binding to use when you want to add more depth and colour to the edge of a quilt, but don't want to add a border, and is what I have used on my sampler quilt. See opposite for the fabric amounts and cutting instructions.

The steps that follow are almost the same as those you would follow for a regular square-corner binding; the only differences are you will need to trim the quilted wadding/batting and backing to extend ¾in (2cm) from the quilt top, and you're left with a wider finished binding.

To make the binding follow the instructions on page 123. You can keep this as a continuous length and cut as you sew.

1 Trim the wadding/batting and backing fabric, leaving a ¾in (2cm) allowance around the quilt top.

2 Sew a strip of binding to one side of the quilt, raw edges matching and with the tape facing towards the centre of the quilt, using the method described left. When you have finished sewing, trim the binding to the size of the wadding/batting and backing fabric. Repeat on the opposite side.

3 Finger press the strips away from the quilt top. Now stitch the remaining strips of binding to the top and bottom of the quilt top. Start by matching the raw edge of the binding to the raw edge of the quilt top, but make sure you start the strip at the fold of the binding already in place. Once the strips are sewn, finger press away from the centre of the quilt top.

4 On the back of the quilt, trim away the surplus backing fabric and wadding/batting from each corner, as shown, to make turning the binding in easier and to reduce bulk.

5 Starting in the middle of a straight side, turn the binding over to the back of the quilt and pin in place along the line of stitching made from attaching the binding to the front of the quilt (see the dashed green line). As you approach the corner, fold the binding so it encases the raw edge. Pin in place and repeat at each corner.

6 Slip stitch the binding in place, stitching down each end/corner completely to secure it.

Quantities needed for sampler quilt

▸ **Overall fabric needed:** 36in (91.5cm) x WOF

▸ **Binding strips:** cut eight strips 4½in (11.5cm) wide x WOF long.

Join the strips to make a continuous length (see page 123); this prevents unnecessary bulk when folding over. Fold along the length WS together and press.

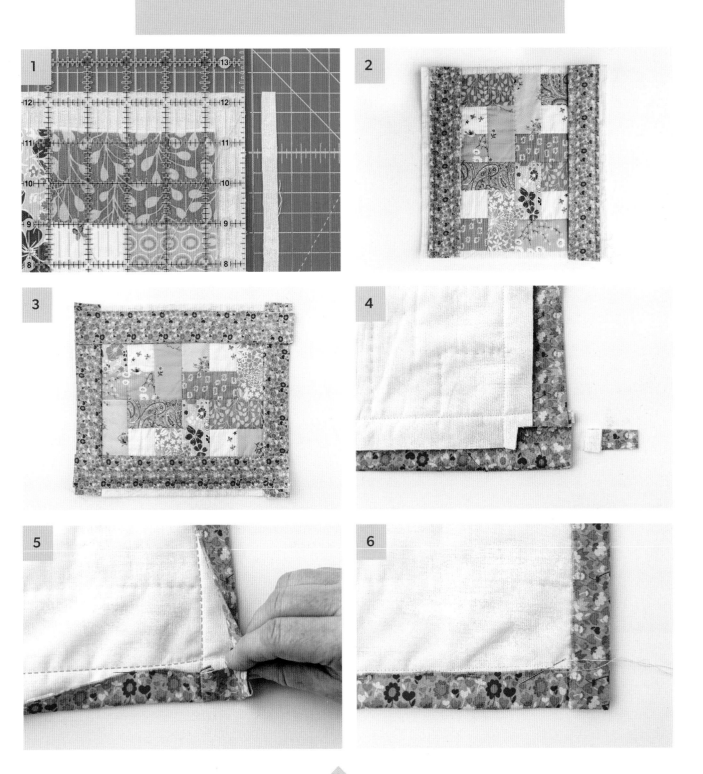

ALTERNATIVE BINDING METHODS

Quantities needed for sampler quilt

- **Overall fabric needed:** 20in (55cm) x WOF
- **Binding strips:** cut eight strips 2½in (6.25cm) wide x WOF long. Join the strips to make a continuous length (see page 123). Fold along the length WS together and press.

Continuous mitred binding

This is a more traditional way to bind the quilt, leaving it with a narrow binding of approximately ⅜in (1cm) wide. If you bind your quilt this way, trim the backing and wadding/batting in line with the patchwork top on the front of the quilt, or you can leave the excess and trim it off when the binding has been applied.

1 To start, make the mock bias join at one end of your binding. Fold over one end of the strip by 90 degrees.

2 Trim off the excess fabric at the end of the strip, leaving a ¼in (5mm) seam allowance.

3 Pin the binding to the quilt top, about one-third of the way along one edge and raw edges aligned. Start with the end with the mock bias join. Sew the binding along the edge with a ¼in (5mm) seam allowance, as per page 124, then stop ¼in (5mm) from the first corner you meet.

4 Fold the binding at a 90-degree angle, away from the quilt and so the free long edge of the binding aligns with the next, unbound edge of the quilt.

5 Fold the binding back down along the next unbound edge, aligning the raw edges and creating a fold at the corner. Start sewing from the folded edge. Sew down to the next corner, and repeat to sew the rest of the binding to the quilt top.

6 When you have stitched all the way around the quilt, trim the binding at an angle and so it overlaps the starting (mock bias join) end by about ⅜in (1cm). Tuck the trimmed end inside the end with the mock bias join. Then, continue to stitch along the binding as before to secure the ends to the quilt top.

7 Trim the excess wadding/batting (if you haven't already) then turn the binding over to the back of the quilt. The corners should 'magically' mitre. Pin the binding, so the folded edge covers your stitching, then slip stitch in place along the fold. You will need to stitch the mitred corners closed, to stop them from opening.

Self-bound binding

This is a lovely method to stitch by hand, and no extra fabric is needed as you use the surplus backing fabric around the edge of your quilt to create binding. You may want to consider which fabric you choose for the backing if you are using this method, as it will show on the front of the quilt.

1 After quilting, trim the wadding/batting to the size of the quilt top, then trim the backing fabric so it's ¾in (2cm) larger than the quilt top and wadding/batting.

2 Starting in the middle of a straight side, turn the backing over so the raw edge touches the raw edge of the trimmed quilt. Fold over the backing once more, so that it covers the raw edge of the quilt top.

3 Repeat with the rest of the backing, round the whole quilt top. The corners should 'step', overlapping the previously folded edge as shown. Pin in place as you work.

4 Slip stitch the folded backing to the quilt top, along the fold. The stitches should not go through to the back of the quilt, but will be worked through the quilt top and wadding/batting. Start in the middle of a straight edge, coming up through the wadding/batting to hide the waste knot and tail behind the backing/binding. At the corners, stitch down each end/corner completely to secure it.

Big-stitch binding

To do this, use the method for continous binding (see opposite) but apply the binding from the BACK of the quilt. This way, when you turn the folded edge over to secure the binding, the big-stitch quilting holding it in place will be on the front of the quilt.

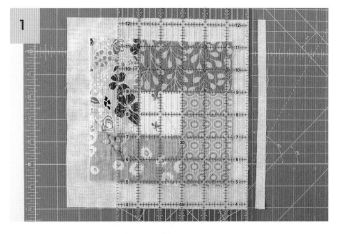

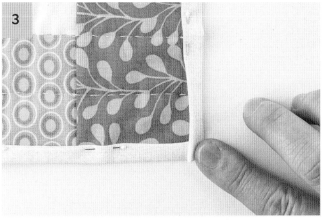

HAND MADE BY
Carolyn Forster

LABELLING & AFTERCARE

LABELLING YOUR QUILT

Once your quilt is sewn and bound, it's worth giving a thought to labelling it – especially when it has been made entirely by hand, over a long period of time. Quilts are designed to last a very long time, and a label bearing your name and the date will serve as an enduring reminder of your quilt's origins. If it is for a gift, you can add a short message and perhaps the recipient's name too.

Handwritten

The labelling can be written directly on to the back of the quilt with a permanent marker pen, or on to a calico or muslin label that is then stitched to the quilt.

Pre-printed labels

Many craft shops sell fabrics consisting of decorative blank labels. Buy these by the metre or yard to cut out and use on your projects. Labels can also be ordered from name-tape suppliers, and you can customize these with various motifs and phrases.

Embroidered & cross-stitched labels

Many talented quilters embroider too. Consider embellishing your written label with simple stitching such as backstitch. With a little planning and some graph paper, you can work a cross-stitch label. A special canvas, known as waste canvas, can be used on top of the calico and the threads pulled away afterwards to leave your stitching on the calico.

Printed computer labels

If writing your label is proving a little daunting, then you can produce one on the computer instead. Simply create your label as a document and then print it out on to special fabric sheets. Just follow the instructions to make the printing permanent, and stitch the label to the quilt.

LAUNDERING QUILTS

Once your quilt is finished, it may need laundering. This will freshen the quilt after so much handling and remove any markings that were made during the quilting. Also, depending on the wadding/batting used, laundering will shrink the quilt a little and emphasize the quilting stitches.

Quilts are quite sturdy and can easily be washed in a washing machine. Only antique and fragile quilts are best washed by hand. I put my quilts in the machine on a gentle cycle at 30°C (86°F) with detergent specially formulated for colours. If you are concerned about colour bleeding, put in a few 'colour catchers'.

On a windy day I will dry the quilt on a clothes line outside. If I cannot do that then I will put it in the tumble dryer long enough to take out the excess water, then I put it in the airing cupboard or over a clothes airer. Once the quilt is dry it can be used straight away – it will not need ironing.

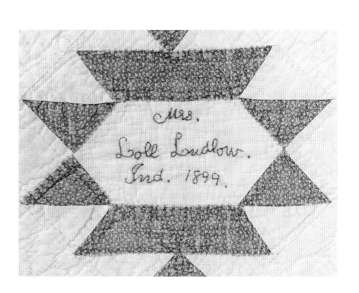

PATCHWORK TEMPLATES

Free templates

These templates are also available to download free from the Bookmarked Hub website:

www.bookmarkedhub.com

Search for this book by title or ISBN: the files can be found under 'Book Extras'. Membership of the Bookmarked online community is free.

Every block has templates, all of which are provided at 100% scale on the following pages. Note that SAs are not included, and will need to be added where necessary. For templates that have the letter 'R' included in the name, this stands for 'reflect' and means you will need to flip the template to create a mirror image. Refer to each block's 'Cut' details for information on cutting quantities. All the templates in the book will feature a grain line arrow, indicating the direction the templates will need placed in before cutting around them.

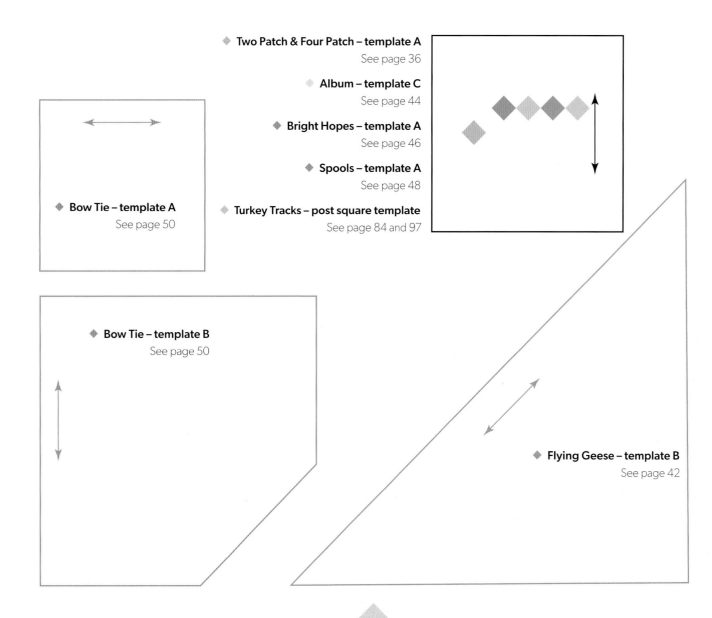

Two Patch & Four Patch – template A
See page 36

Album – template C
See page 44

Bright Hopes – template A
See page 46

Spools – template A
See page 48

Turkey Tracks – post square template
See page 84 and 97

Bow Tie – template A
See page 50

Bow Tie – template B
See page 50

Flying Geese – template B
See page 42

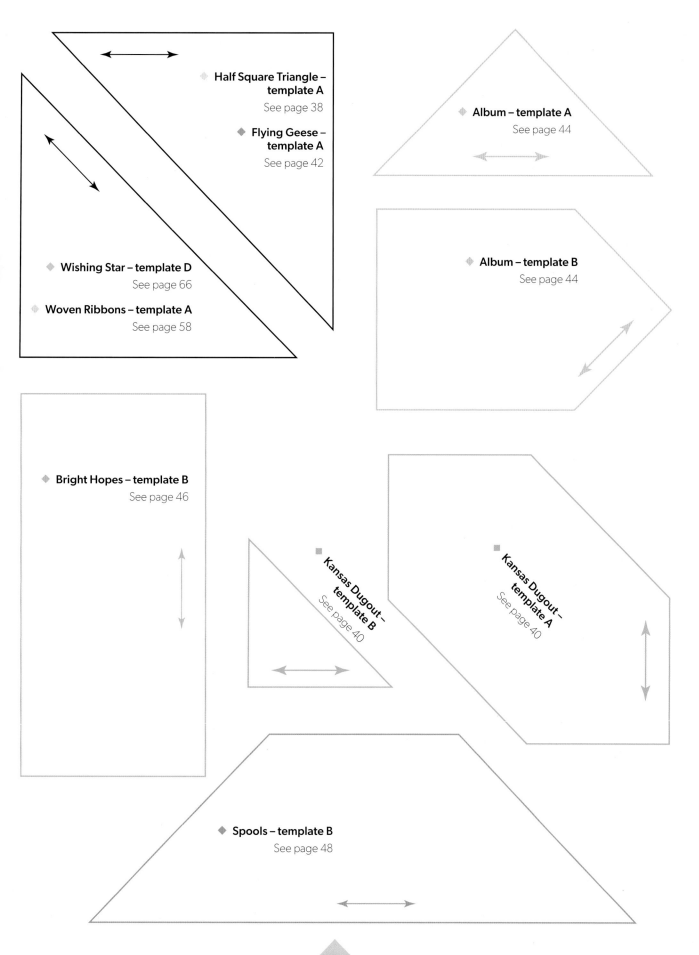

Half Square Triangle –
template A
See page 38

Flying Geese –
template A
See page 42

Album – template A
See page 44

Album – template B
See page 44

Wishing Star – template D
See page 66

Woven Ribbons – template A
See page 58

Bright Hopes – template B
See page 46

Kansas Dugout –
template B
See page 40

Kansas Dugout –
template A
See page 40

Spools – template B
See page 48

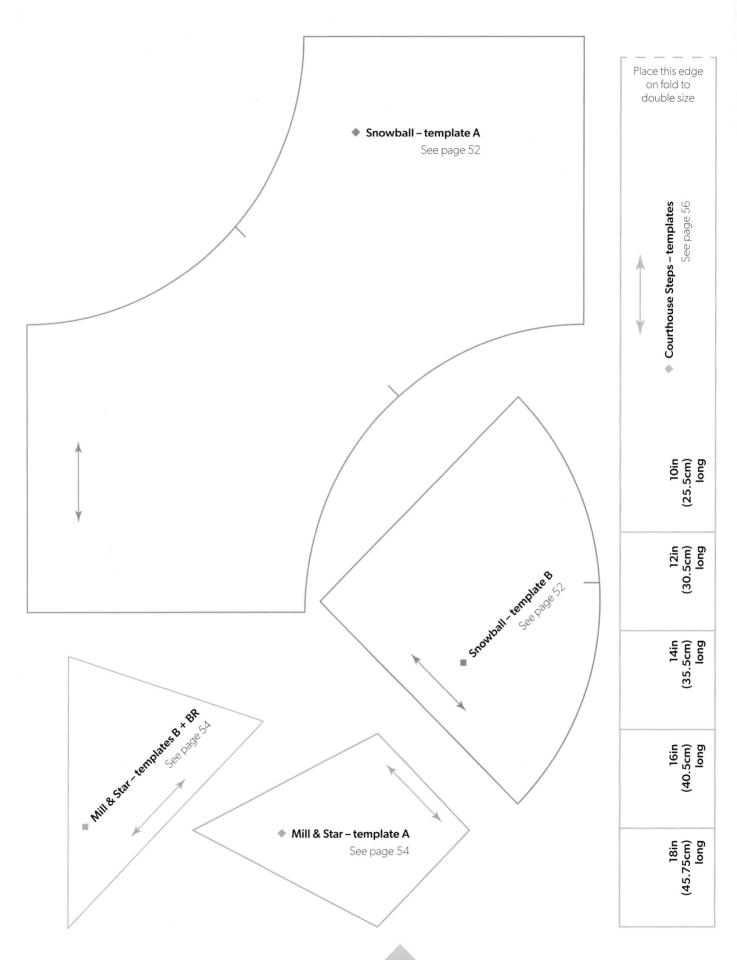

◆ **Snowball – template A**
See page 52

Place this edge
on fold to
double size

Courthouse Steps – templates
See page 56

10in
(25.5cm)
long

12in
(30.5cm)
long

■ **Snowball – template B**
See page 52

14in
(35.5cm)
long

16in
(40.5cm)
long

Mill & Star – templates B + BR
See page 54

◆ **Mill & Star – template A**
See page 54

18in
(45.75cm)
long

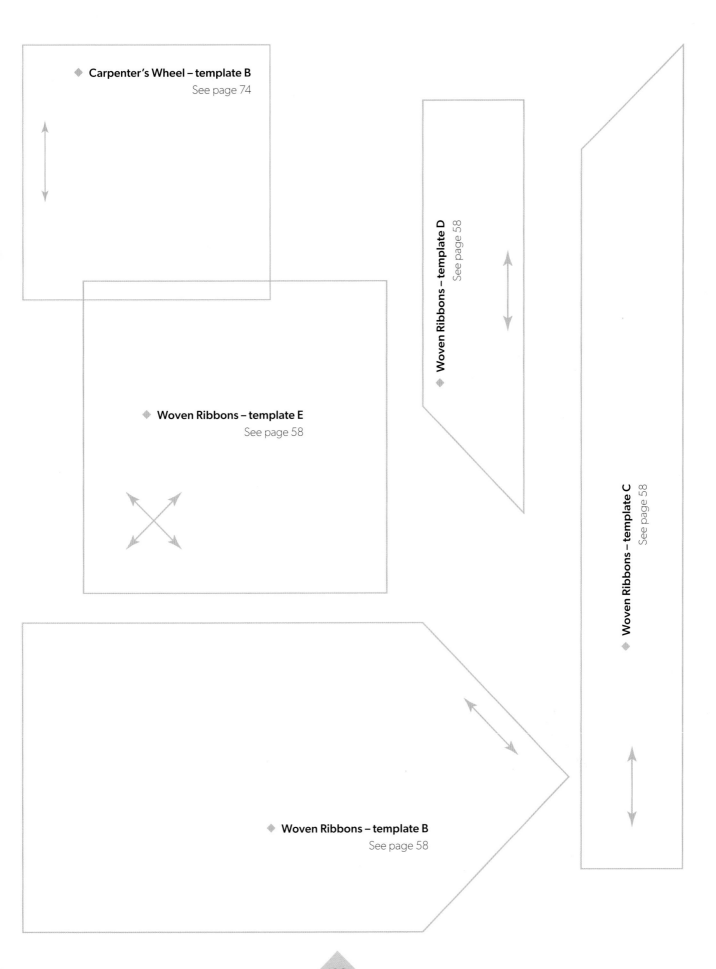

◆ **Carpenter's Wheel – template B**
See page 74

◆ **Woven Ribbons – template E**
See page 58

◆ **Woven Ribbons – template D**
See page 58

◆ **Woven Ribbons – template C**
See page 58

◆ **Woven Ribbons – template B**
See page 58

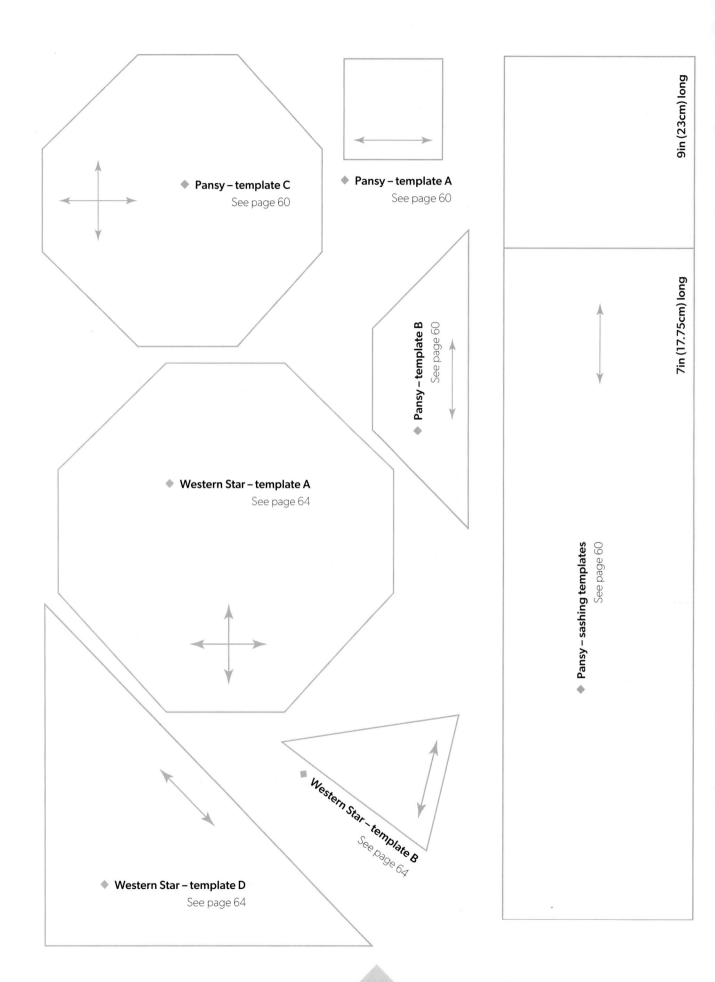

◆ **Pansy – template C**
See page 60

◆ **Pansy – template A**
See page 60

◆ **Pansy – template B**
See page 60

◆ **Western Star – template A**
See page 64

9in (23cm) long

7in (17.75cm) long

◆ **Pansy – sashing templates**
See page 60

Western Star – template B
See page 64

◆ **Western Star – template D**
See page 64

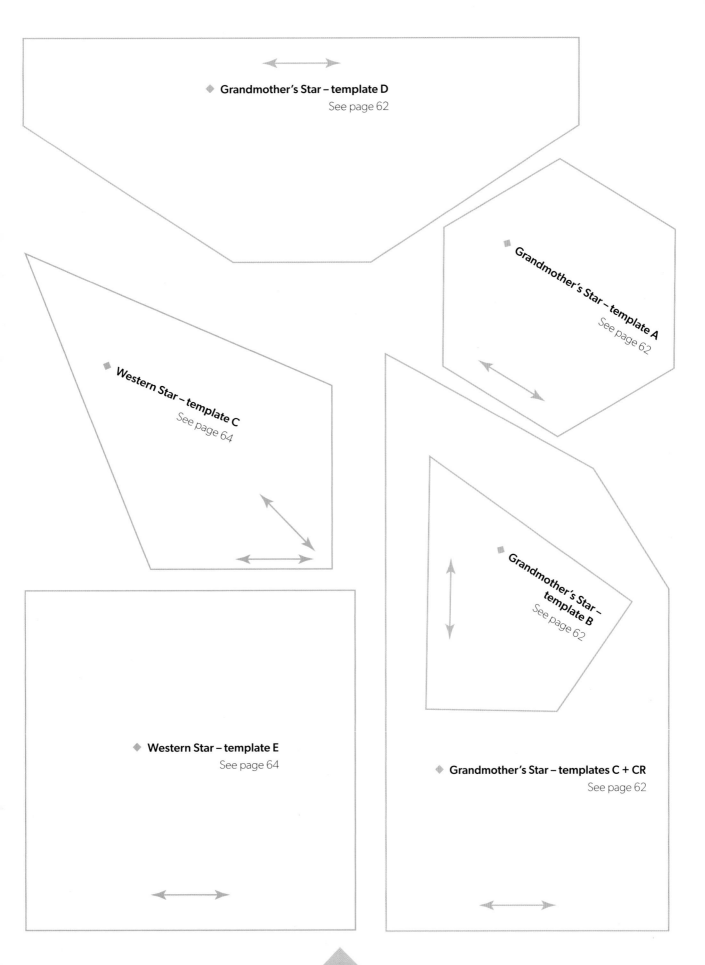

Grandmother's Star – template D
See page 62

Grandmother's Star – template A
See page 62

Western Star – template C
See page 64

Grandmother's Star – template B
See page 62

Western Star – template E
See page 64

Grandmother's Star – templates C + CR
See page 62

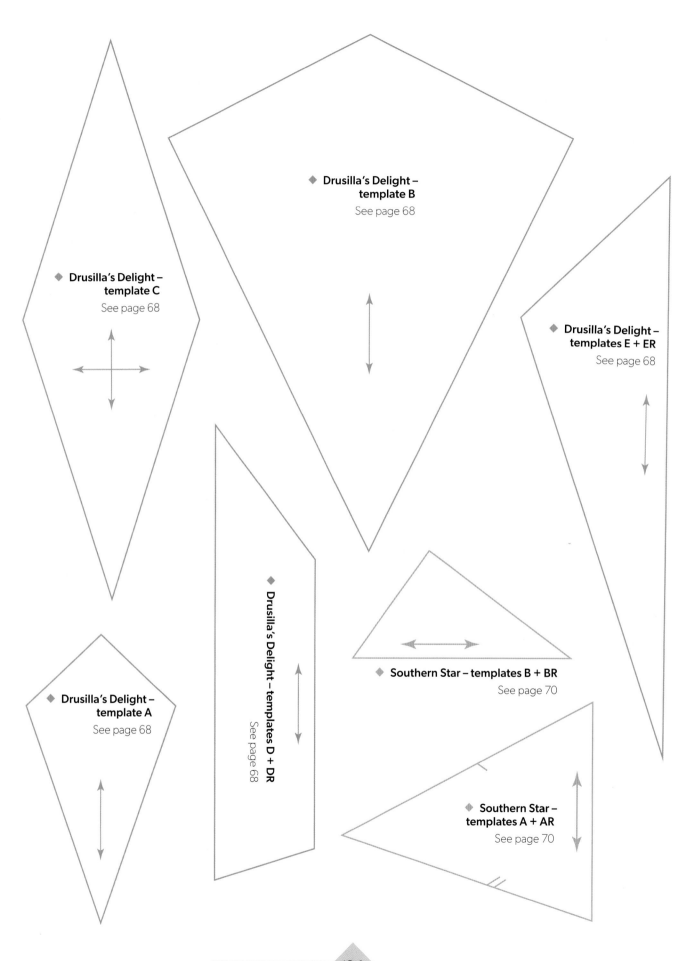

◆ **Drusilla's Delight – template B**
See page 68

◆ **Drusilla's Delight – template C**
See page 68

◆ **Drusilla's Delight – templates E + ER**
See page 68

◆ **Drusilla's Delight – templates D + DR**
See page 68

◆ **Drusilla's Delight – template A**
See page 68

◆ **Southern Star – templates B + BR**
See page 70

◆ **Southern Star – templates A + AR**
See page 70

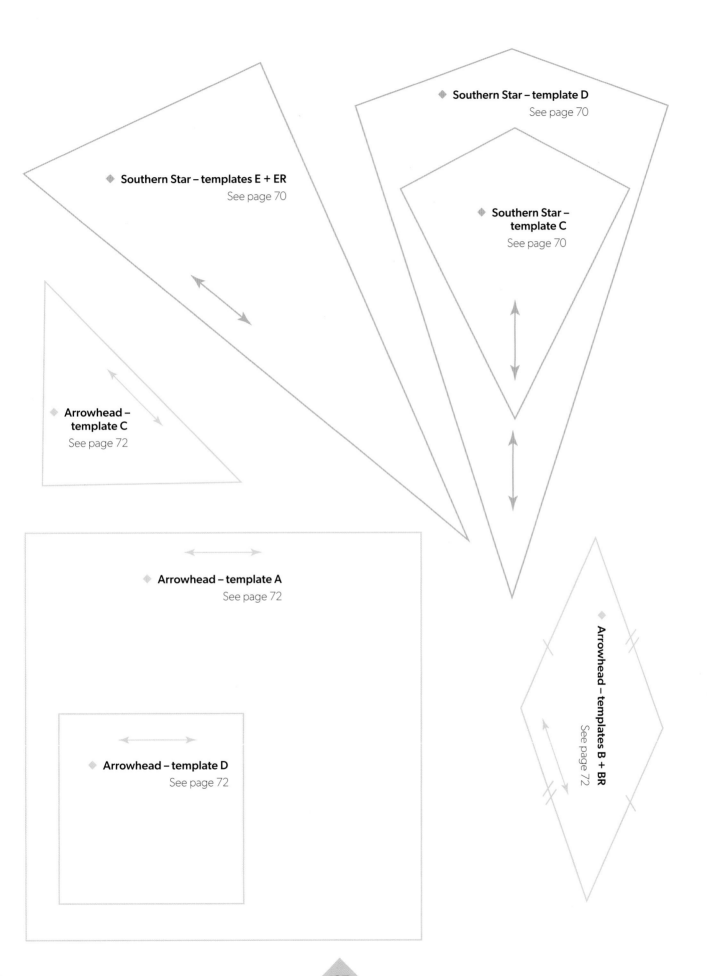

Southern Star – templates E + ER
See page 70

Southern Star – template D
See page 70

Southern Star – template C
See page 70

Arrowhead – template C
See page 72

Arrowhead – template A
See page 72

Arrowhead – template D
See page 72

Arrowhead – templates B + BR
See page 72

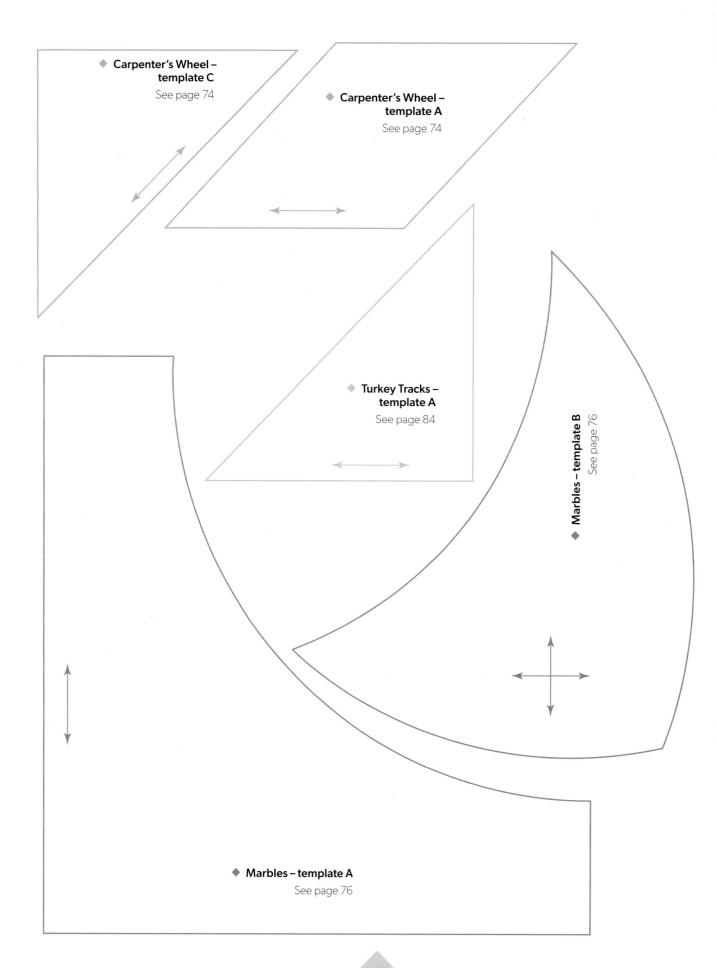

◆ **Carpenter's Wheel – template C**
See page 74

◆ **Carpenter's Wheel – template A**
See page 74

◆ **Turkey Tracks – template A**
See page 84

◆ **Marbles – template B**
See page 76

◆ **Marbles – template A**
See page 76

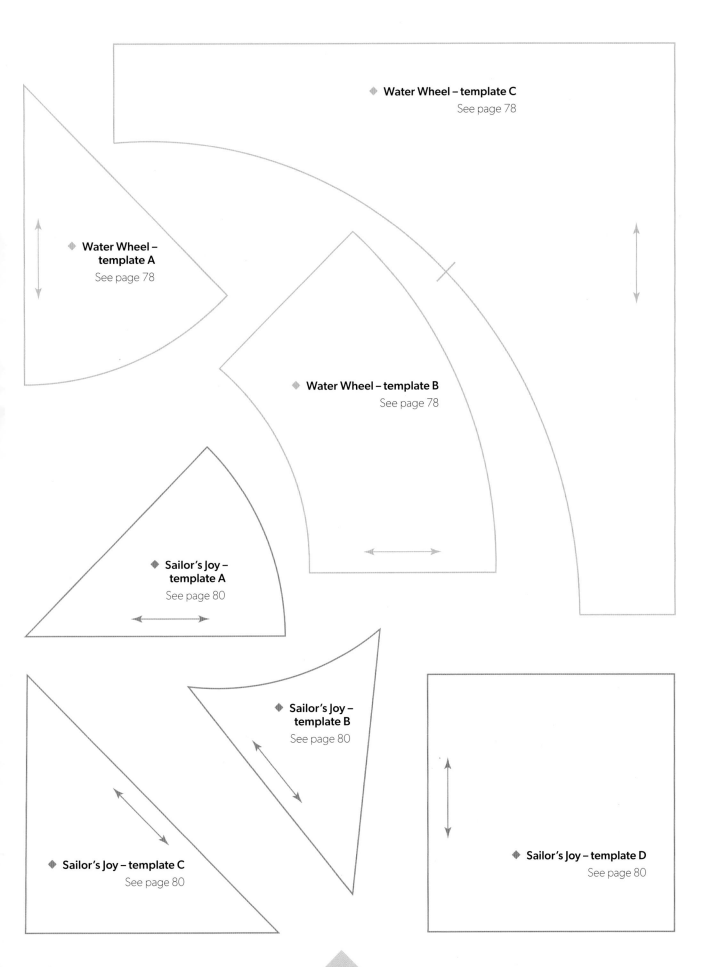

Water Wheel – template C
See page 78

Water Wheel – template A
See page 78

Water Wheel – template B
See page 78

Sailor's Joy – template A
See page 80

Sailor's Joy – template B
See page 80

Sailor's Joy – template C
See page 80

Sailor's Joy – template D
See page 80

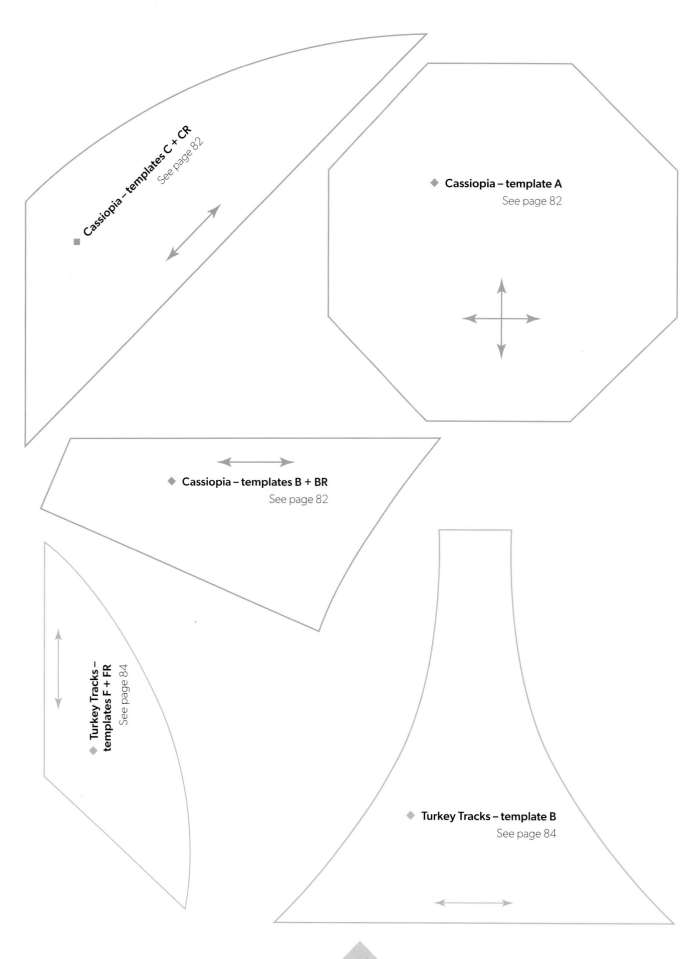

Cassiopia – templates C + CR
See page 82

◆ **Cassiopia – template A**
See page 82

◆ **Cassiopia – templates B + BR**
See page 82

◆ **Turkey Tracks – templates F + FR**
See page 84

◆ **Turkey Tracks – template B**
See page 84

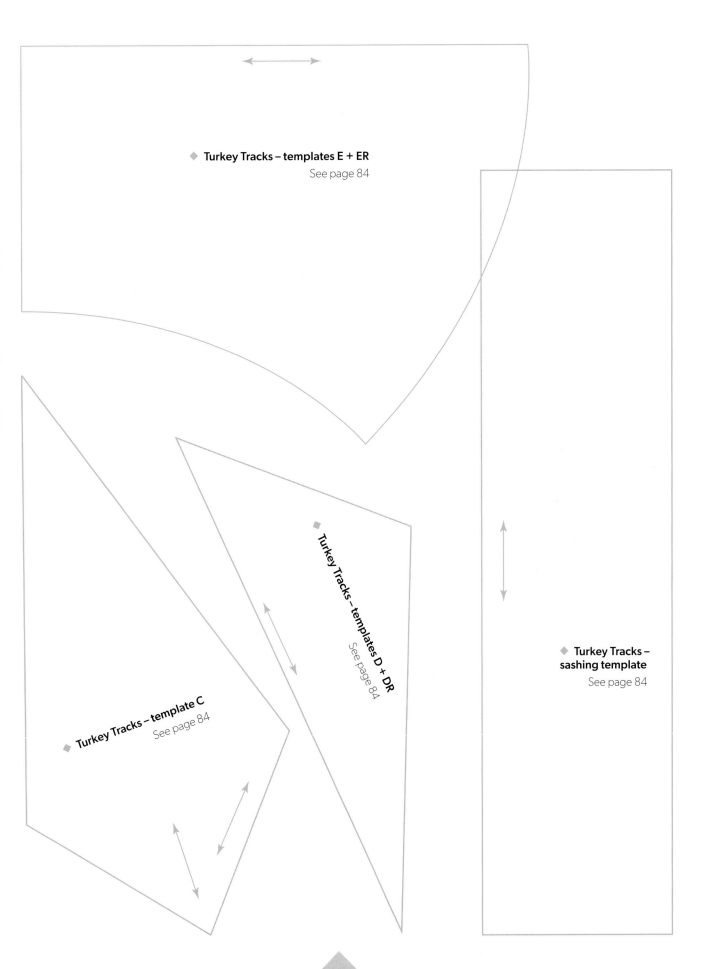

◆ **Turkey Tracks – templates E + ER**
See page 84

Turkey Tracks – templates D + DR
See page 84

Turkey Tracks – template C
See page 84

◆ **Turkey Tracks – sashing template**
See page 84

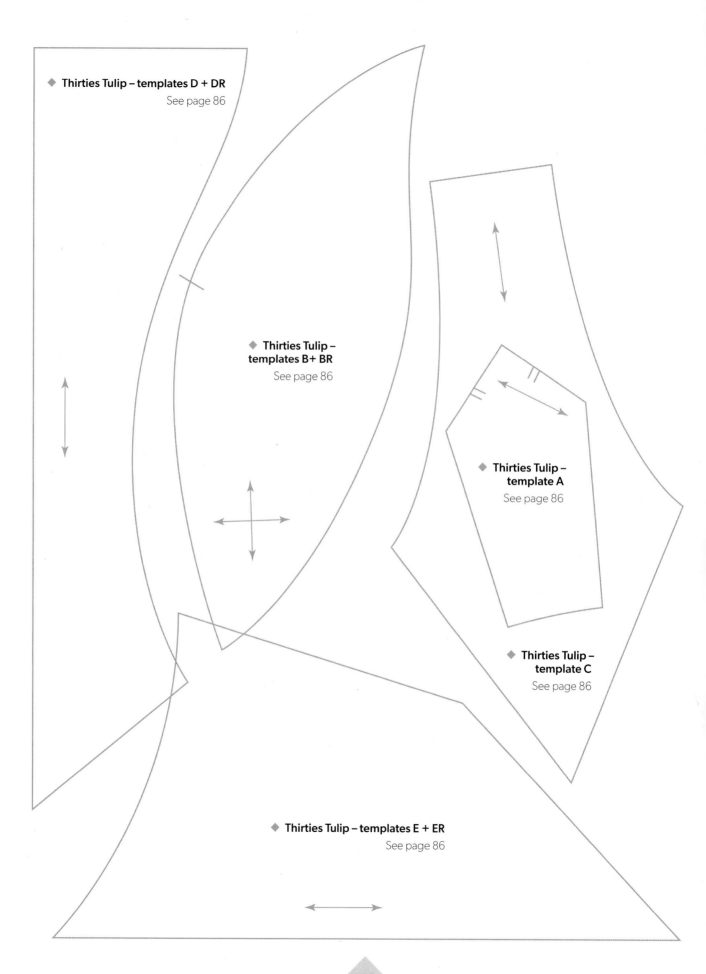

◆ **Thirties Tulip – templates D + DR**
See page 86

◆ **Thirties Tulip – templates B+ BR**
See page 86

◆ **Thirties Tulip – template A**
See page 86

◆ **Thirties Tulip – template C**
See page 86

◆ **Thirties Tulip – templates E + ER**
See page 86

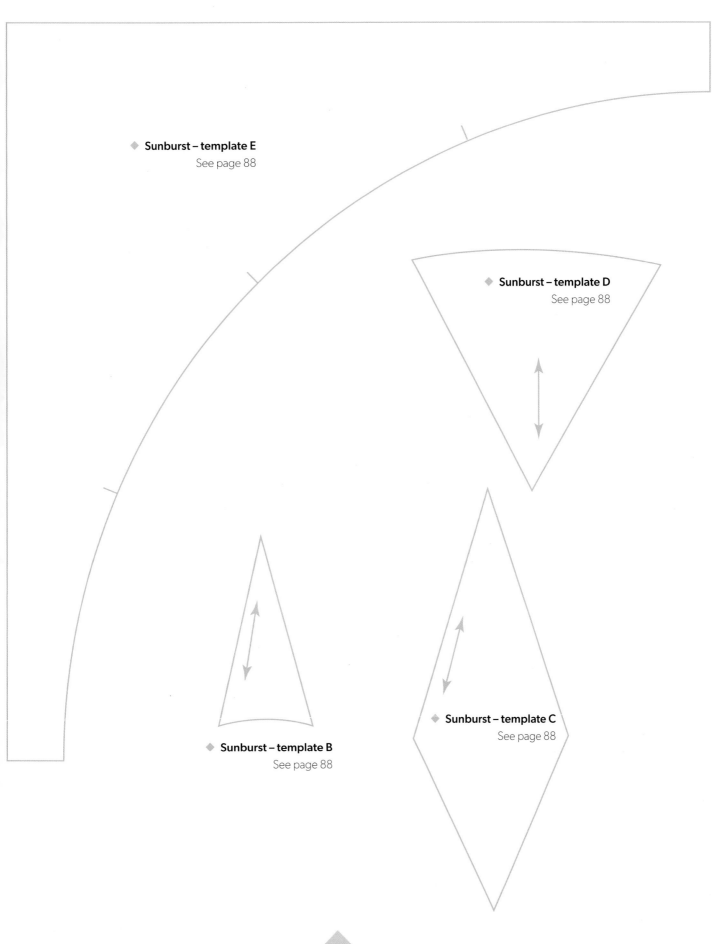

Sunburst – template E
See page 88

Sunburst – template D
See page 88

Sunburst – template B
See page 88

Sunburst – template C
See page 88

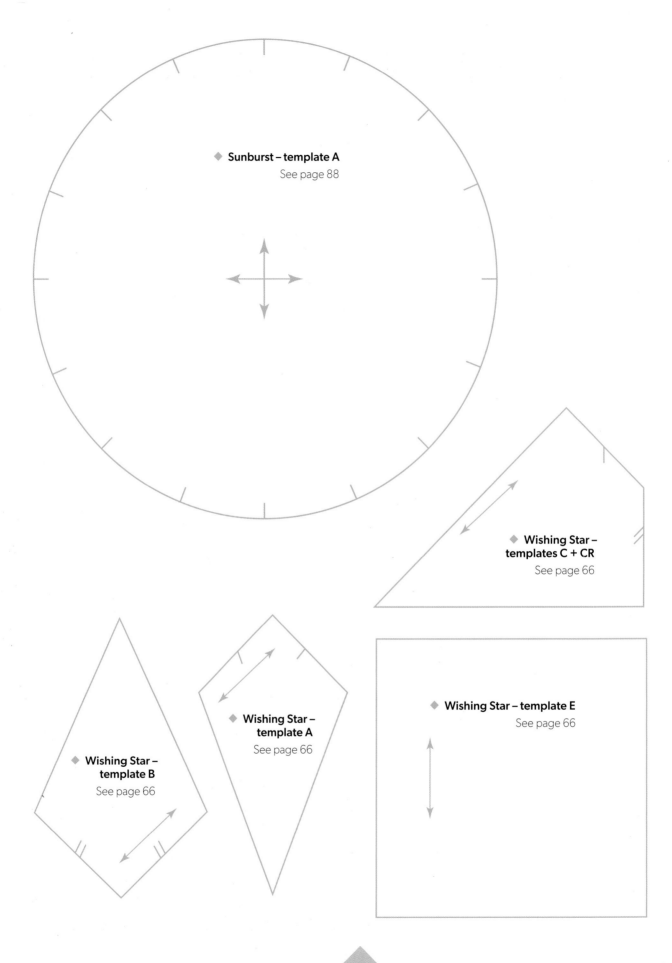

◆ **Sunburst – template A**
See page 88

◆ **Wishing Star –
templates C + CR**
See page 66

◆ **Wishing Star –
template A**
See page 66

◆ **Wishing Star – template E**
See page 66

◆ **Wishing Star –
template B**
See page 66